# My revision planner

REVISED

## Unit 2 Outline study

**International Relations, 1945–2003**

# Features to help you succeed

### What you need to know

These boxes quickly summarise what you should know when you have finished revising each section. Make sure you know all of this before you tick the heading.

### Revision tasks

These short, knowledge-based questions provide the first step in testing your learning.

### Exam practice

Sample exam questions are provided for each topic. Use them to consolidate your revision and practice your exam skills.

### Key terms

Key terms are highlighted the first time they appear. You can find the definitions in the glossary online.

### Online

Go online to check your answers to the Exam practice questions and to find the glossary of key terms at **www.hoddereducation.co.uk/myrevisionnotesdownloads**

# my **revision** notes

# CCEA GCSE
# HISTORY

Finbar Madden
Rob Quinn

HODDER
EDUCATION
AN HACHETTE UK COMPANY

3 8015 02571 602 2

The Publishers would like to thank the following for permission to reproduce copyright material.

**Photo credits**

**p. 69** © Windows To Ireland; **p. 163** © Carlos Latuff via Wikipedia (released into the public domain)

**Acknowledgements**

**p. 34** Exam practice question 1, Exam practice question 2 © CCEA; **p. 41** Exam practice question 3 © CCEA; **p. 47** Exam practice question 4, Exam practice question 5 © CCEA; **p. 113** Exam practice question 2 © CCEA; **p. 128** Exam practice question 5 © CCEA; **p. 129** Exam practice question 6, Exam practice question 7 © CCEA

Every effort has been made to trace all copyright holders, but if any have been inadvertently overlooked, the Publishers will be pleased to make the necessary arrangements at the first opportunity.

Although every effort has been made to ensure that website addresses are correct at time of going to press, Hodder Education cannot be held responsible for the content of any website mentioned in this book. It is sometimes possible to find a relocated web page by typing in the address of the home page for a website in the URL window of your browser.

Hachette UK's policy is to use papers that are natural, renewable and recyclable products and made from wood grown in sustainable forests. The logging and manufacturing processes are expected to conform to the environmental regulations of the country of origin.

Orders: please contact Bookpoint Ltd, 130 Park Drive, Milton Park, Abingdon, Oxon OX14 4SE. Telephone: +44 (0)1235 827827. Fax: +44 (0)1235 400401. Email education@bookpoint.co.uk Lines are open from 9 a.m. to 5 p.m., Monday to Saturday, with a 24-hour message answering service. You can also order through our website: www.hoddereducation.co.uk

ISBN: 978 1 4718 8977 6

© Finbar Madden and Rob Quinn 2018

First published in 2018 by

Hodder Education,

An Hachette UK Company

Carmelite House

50 Victoria Embankment

London EC4Y 0DZ

www.hoddereducation.co.uk

Impression number    10 9 8 7 6 5 4 3 2 1

Year        2022 2021 2020 2019 2018

All rights reserved. Apart from any use permitted under UK copyright law, no part of this publication may be reproduced or transmitted in any form or by any means, electronic or mechanical, including photocopying and recording, or held within any information storage and retrieval system, without permission in writing from the publisher or under licence from the Copyright Licensing Agency Limited. Further details of such licences (for reprographic reproduction) may be obtained from the Copyright Licensing Agency Limited, www.cla.co.uk
Cover photo ©Markus Matzel/ullstein bild/Getty Images
Illustrations by Aptara Inc.
Typeset in India by Aptara Inc.
Printed in Spain by Graphycems

A catalogue record for this title is available from the British Library.

# Introduction

## About the course

The course you are studying is split into two units: Unit 1, a Modern world depth study and a Local study, and Unit 2, the Outline study. There are four options in Unit 1. You only need to study two of the options, one from Section A and one from Section B. The whole of Unit 2 is compulsory.

### Unit 1 Section A: Modern world depth study

Option 1: Life under Nazi dictatorship, 1933–1945
or
Option 2: Life in the United States of America, 1920–33

### Unit 1 Section B: Local study

Option 1: Changing Relations: Northern Ireland and its Neighbours, 1920–49
or
Option 2: Changing Relations: Northern Ireland and its Neighbours, 1965–1998

### Unit 2: Outline study

International Relations, 1945–2003

## The examination

There are two papers in the examination. Paper 1 covers the Modern World Depth Study and the Local Study, while Paper 2 focuses on the Outline Study.

### Revision techniques

Whatever your revision style, there are a number of practical suggestions as to how you should approach revision and use your time:
- Start your revision in plenty of time.
- Organise a revision timetable for each section of the course.
- Draw up a revision checklist that allows you to focus on the parts of the course that you are most concerned about.
- Set yourself a target of material to cover in each session – for example, Nazi attempts to reduce unemployment – and stick to it.
- Revise for short periods – 15–20 minutes, for example – and take breaks in between.
- Review what you have covered at the end of the day and again the next day to make sure you have internalised the information.
- Be open to using a range of ways of remembering material. For example, rhymes, mnemonics, coding and diagrams.
- Consult all relevant CCEA Mark Schemes and Chief Examiner's Reports to see what the examiners are looking for and – more importantly – the mistakes that they want you to avoid.
- Leave yourself enough time to revisit material that you have already revised closer to the time of the examination.

# Sitting the examination

## General points

- Make sure you're **looking at the right questions**. This is particularly relevant to the two Northern Ireland sections in Paper 1.
- Look for **all of the questions** – some may be over the page. Don't forget to check!
- Follow the **instructions** on the front of the exam paper - and within each section.
- **Read** each question carefully – ideally more than once.
- Use a highlighter pen to emphasise **key points/words** in a question.
- Answer the question that has been set – not the one you wish had been set!
- Remember the connection between the amount of marks for each question and how much you are expected to write.
- Stick rigidly to whatever dates are given in a question.
- If you want to score strongly in each part of the examination, you must spend the appropriate amount of time on each question. Too much time spent on one section will mean too little left for others.
- Stay for the **full amount** of time. You can't get marks if you're not there!

## Timing

You should spend no more than the amount of time suggested below on each question part.

### Paper 1: Section A

| Question | Mark | Suggested timing |
| --- | --- | --- |
| Question 1 | 4 marks | 4 minutes |
| Question 2 | 6 marks | 5 minutes |
| Question 3 | 6 marks | 5–7 minutes |
| Question 4 | 8 marks | 10 minutes |
| Question 5 | 16 marks | 15–20 minutes |

### Paper 1: Section B

| Question | Mark | Timing |
| --- | --- | --- |
| Question 1 | 2 marks | 2–3 minutes |
| Question 2 | 4 marks | 5–6 minutes |
| Question 3 | 5 marks | 5–7 minutes |
| Question 4 | 6 marks | 6–8 minutes |
| Question 5 | 5 marks | 4 minutes |
| Question 6 | 18 marks | 20 minutes |

### Paper 2

| Question | Mark | Timing |
| --- | --- | --- |
| Question 1 | 4 marks | 5 minutes |
| Question 2a | 4 marks | 5 minutes |
| Question 2b | 2 marks | 3 minutes |
| Question 3 | 8 marks | 10 minutes |
| Question 4 | 16 marks | 20 minutes |
| Question 5 | 4 marks | 5 minutes |
| Question 6 | 22 marks | 25 minutes |

## Remember!

- Your answers must demonstrate a detailed knowledge. This book provides you with the key facts on each topic. Learn these thoroughly!
- Structure your answer. Most frequently a chronological framework will be the best way to achieve this.
- Select appropriate facts to answer the question asked.
- Many pupils lose marks by failing to identify all relevant information. Instead of writing a lot about one point, try to write less about a number of points.

Exam practice answers at **www.hoddereducation.co.uk/myrevisionnotesdownloads**

# Option 1 Life under Nazi dictatorship, 1933–45

## 1 Hitler takes political control, 1933–34

### Hitler's appointment as Chancellor

REVISED

#### Weimar Germany, 1919-33

In the 1920s, Germany was known as the Weimar Republic. Though the Republic had a President, real power was held by the elected *Reichstag*. It was weak and was constantly attacked by:
- **Communists**
- right wing groups, such as the Nazi Party (NSDAP).

#### The rise of the Nazis

The Nazi Party encouraged violence and hatred and wanted to return Germany to her pre-First World War military strength. It had the support of the **SS** and the SA.

The Nazis gained popularity in Germany when the 1929 Great Depression led to an increase in their support from Germany's working and middle classes. This led to:
- 230 Nazi deputies being elected to the *Reichstag* in July 1932
- a destabilisation of the *Reichstag*
- the president von Hindenburg and former Chancellor von Papen offering Hitler the post of Chancellor in a **coalition** government.

Hitler finally accepted the position of Chancellor in January 1933.

#### The removal of opposition

To achieve dictatorship Hitler would have to overcome the President, the *Reichstag* and the Army. In addition, there might be opposition from other parties, Germany's **state governments** or its **trade unions**.

To gain a majority in the *Reichstag*, Hitler called fresh elections for 5 March 1933. To achieve this majority, he had to stop people voting for the **SPD** and **KPD**. Therefore:
- in early February a new law forbade newspapers and public meetings from criticising Hitler and his government
- in the state of Prussia, **SA** members were enrolled into the police and were used to disrupt opposition parties' election campaigns.

> **What you need to know**
>
> You need to be able to explain how the instability of the Weimar **Republic** and the **Great Depression** allowed the **Nazi Party** to grow in popularity, so much that Hitler was able to become Chancellor in January 1933.

# The *Reichstag* Fire

REVISED

Dutch Communist, Marinus van der Lubbe, was captured at the burning *Reichstag* building on 27 February. His arrest helped Hitler to destroy the KPD's election campaign by exploiting fears of a Communist revolution. However, some people suspected that the Nazis set the fire to gain a political advantage as Hitler used the fire to persuade the President to approve the Decree for the Protection of People and State.

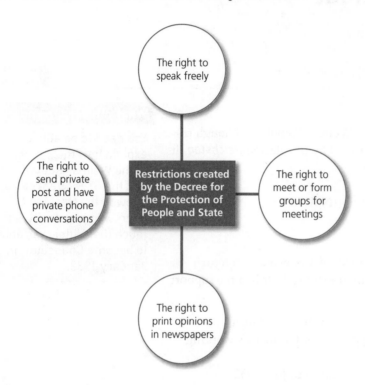

This immediately enabled the Nazis to intimidate and imprison their opponents.

**What you need to know**

You should be able to understand how the *Reichstag* Fire enabled Hitler to play on von Hindenburg's fear of a Communist revolution.

## Revision tasks

1 How do we know Germany was in difficulty before 1933?
2 Create a spider diagram showing the possible sources of opposition to Hitler after he became Chancellor.
3 Make notes about the *Reichstag* Fire under the following headings:
   ● Date
   ● How Hitler used the fire to his advantage
   ● What the decree for the Protection of the People and State allowed the Nazis to do.

TESTED

# The election of 5 March 1933

REVISED

The 1933 election took place six days after the *Reichstag* Fire. The Nazis used lots of tactics to ensure they got as many votes as possible. These included:

● propaganda
● intimidation – forcing many SPD leaders to flee Germany
● imprisonment of KPD members and trade unionists
● a 'shooting decree' in Prussia.

The results revealed that the Nazis had won 288 seats – too few for an overall majority. However, with the support of 52 Nationalist Party deputies, the Nazis could count on just over 50 per cent of the votes in the *Reichstag*.

**What you need to know**

You must be able to explain how the March 1933 election left the Nazis in a stronger position.

# The Enabling Act, 23 March 1933

Hitler now moved to amend the **constitution** to allow the government to introduce laws without *Reichstag* approval for four years. This change needed the support of two-thirds of the *Reichstag* members present.

To achieve this majority, Hitler:
- used the decree For the Protection of People and State to ban the KPD
- convinced the Catholic **Centre Party (ZP)** to vote for the Act by promising to cancel the decree For the Protection of the People and State and agreeing to protect the rights of the Catholic Church.

The final vote was passed by 441 votes to 94; only the SDP opposed.

> **What you need to know**
>
> You must be able to explain exactly how the Enabling Act allowed the government to introduce laws without the *Reichstag's* approval for a period of four years.

## *Gleichschaltung*

Hitler's government eliminated most of the remaining political opposition in Germany by a process known as *Gleichschaltung*.

> **What you need to know**
>
> Gleichschaltung removed all remaining political opposition to the Nazi party, leading to total political control. Can you explain how?

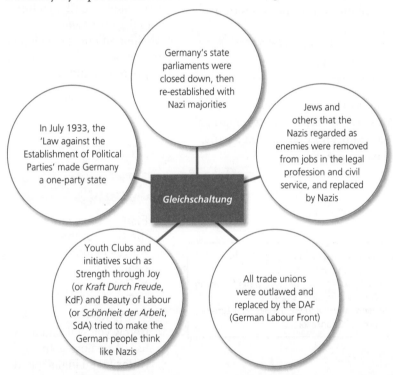

In July 1933, the 'Law against the Establishment of Political Parties' made Germany a one-party state

Germany's state parliaments were closed down, then re-established with Nazi majorities

Jews and others that the Nazis regarded as enemies were removed from jobs in the legal profession and civil service, and replaced by Nazis

*Gleichschaltung*

Youth Clubs and initiatives such as Strength through Joy (or *Kraft Durch Freude*, KdF) and Beauty of Labour (or *Schönheit der Arbeit*, SdA) tried to make the German people think like Nazis

All trade unions were outlawed and replaced by the DAF (German Labour Front)

> **Revision task**
>
> Make a table with three columns about the Enabling Act, using the following headings:
> - Why Hitler wanted it
> - How it was passed
> - What it meant – in terms of how Germany was governed
>
> TESTED

In the November 1933 *Reichstag* elections the Nazis won 92 per cent of the vote.

In January 1934, the Law for the Reconstruction of the State abolished all of Germany's state governments, apart from Prussia's, which continued to be run by leading Nazi and Minister for the Interior Hermann Göring.

## The threat from Röhm and the SA

Hitler's position was still under threat; however, now the danger came from the two-million strong SA, commanded by Ernst Röhm.

Röhm's plans for the SA to replace the Army worried it and Hitler.
- Hitler feared the Army. It was the only group that could stop his achievement of dictatorship.
- He needed the Army to implement his foreign policy aims.

Röhm was also opposed by other leading Nazis such as Heinrich Himmler (SS leader) and Göring.

> **What you need to know**
>
> You should be able to explain just how Röhm expected Hitler's take-over would be followed by a second revolution in which the Army would be crushed and the SA would become Germany's new army.

# The Night of the Long Knives

REVISED

On 30 June 1934, the 'Night of the Long Knives', those suspected of preventing Hitler's achievement of dictatorship were executed, including Röhm. It is believed around 100–200 people were killed on this night. The Nazis justified their actions by claiming that they had prevented an SA *putsch*.

On 3 July, the *Reichstag* approved a law that made these actions taken legal.

**What you need to know**

You should be able to explain how Hitler removed any remaining political and military threats, including Röhm, in the Night of the Long Knives.

## The death of von Hindenburg: Hitler becomes *Führer*

REVISED

Hindenburg was now the only person standing in the way of Hitler's dictatorship, but he died on 2 August 1934. A day earlier a new law had been passed which merged the jobs of President and Chancellor and created the position of *Führer* and *Reich* Chancellor. Hitler's position as *Führer* was consolidated by:
- the Army – which swore an oath of personal loyalty to the *Führer*
- 90 per cent of the German people – who voted in a **plebiscite** to indicate their approval for Hitler's new position.

Little more than 18 months after his appointment as Chancellor, Hitler had turned Germany into a **totalitarian** state. What was most remarkable was that most of the changes introduced had been implemented legally, using the powers granted by the 1933 Enabling Act.

**What you need to know**

Hitler merged the roles of President and Chancellor into the all-powerful position of Führer, which he took in August 1934. Can you explain how and why?

**1919–33**
Weimar Germany

- Unstable *Reichstag* with opposition from left- and right-wing parties
- Increased support for the Nazi party following the Great Depression, 1929
- von Hindenburg and von Papen offer Hitler the post of Chancellor

**January 1933**
Hitler becomes Chancellor of the *Reichstag*

- The *Reichstag* Fire, February 1933
- Decree for the Protection of People and State, February 1933
- 5 March 1933 Elections
- Enabling Act, March 1933
- *Gleichschaltung*
- The Night of the long Knives, June 1934
- Death of von Hindenburg

**August 1934**
Hitler becomes *Führer*

**Summary diagram:** Hitler takes political control

## Revision tasks

1 Explain the events of the Night of the Long Knives using the following headings:
   - Reasons
   - Events
   - Impact
2 Below you will find a list of weakness that Hitler faced in his quest to become Germany's dictator. Please write a phrase/sentence to explain how he overcame each weakness. Remember – one action may have overcome more than one weakness!
   - *Reichstag*
   - Cabinet
   - Hindenburg
   - Army
   - State governments
   - Other parties
   - SA
   - Trade unions

TESTED

# 2 Control and opposition

## The creation of the police state

REVISED

The Nazis also used Germany's security and justice systems to ensure complete control.

### Himmler, the SS and the *Gestapo*

The SS was responsible for police, security, intelligence and enforcing Nazi race rules. It had three main branches.

SS members were trained in '*Junker* Schools'; there they were told they were the 'master race' and were taught absolute loyalty to Hitler. There were almost 250,000 members of the SS in 1939. As a result of his control of Germany's police and security forces, Himmler had immense power. Some historians have even argued that the SS became so powerful that it became a 'state within a state'.

### The law courts

- The legal system came under state control.
- Hitler set up a special People's Court in 1934 which would give the 'right' verdict on those accused of crimes against the state. Trials had Nazi judges, no juries, and those accused were often simply accused and not allowed to defend themselves.
- It is estimated that up to 1939, the judicial system sentenced nearly a quarter of a million Germans to more than 600,000 years in prison.

### Concentration camps

- The Decree for the Protection of People and State allowed opponents to be arrested and placed in 'protective custody' in **concentration camps**.
- By mid-1934, these camps were being run by a part of the SS known as the Death's Head Units.
- In addition to political prisoners, other groups such as Jews, communists, gypsies, homosexuals, alcoholics and prostitutes were interned.

## The impact of the police state

REVISED

The police state largely controlled the lives of ordinary Germans:
- The promotion of people's community (*Volksgemeinschaft*) taught people loyalty to the state and the *Führer*. Offences such as anti-Nazi graffiti or saying business was bad were reported to the *Gestapo* by informers and offenders could be imprisoned.
- A belief in 'clan responsibility' meant that if one member of a family broke the law, the whole family could be punished for the crime.
- As a result many people did not trust their neighbours.

However, the majority of ordinary Germans did approve of the Nazis' desire to eliminate 'enemies of the state'. The controls made them feel safer and they were willing to join the Nazi Party and follow the new rules.

> **What you need to know**
>
> You need to be able to explain what the police state was and how it worked.

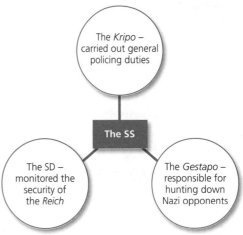

The Kripo – carried out general policing duties

The SS

The SD – monitored the security of the *Reich*

The *Gestapo* – responsible for hunting down Nazi opponents

> **What you need to know**
>
> Examiners will expect you to be able to explain how successful the police state was in controlling the lives of ordinary Germans.

> **Revision tasks**
>
> 1 Create a spider diagram showing the different groups that ended up in concentration camps.
> 2 How successful were the different elements of the police state?
>
> TESTED

# Propaganda and censorship

## Goebbels and Nazi ideas

Gaining support for the Nazis was the job of Dr Josef Goebbels, Minister for Popular Enlightenment and Propaganda. To assist him, Göbbels established the *Reich* Chamber of Culture.

## The Ministry of Propaganda

One of the Nazis' most impressive propaganda methods were the annual Nuremberg rallies. Light, sound and costume were used to create an awe-inspiring atmosphere.

The Ministry also controlled culture in the following ways:
- a 1934 law outlawed anti-Nazi stories and jokes
- 'degenerate' art was unfavourably compared with Nazi realism
- jazz music was condemned as unacceptable
- literature was censored
- films such as *The Eternal Jew* portrayed Jews negatively
- listening to foreign radio broadcasts was banned.

Control of the media – another key aim – was achieved in a variety of ways:

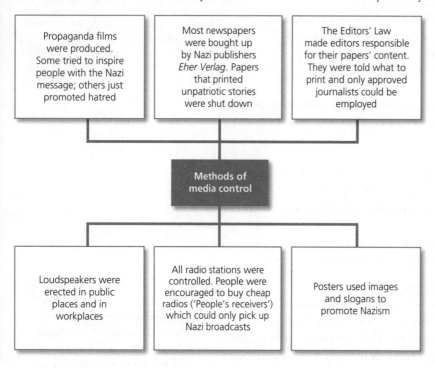

Propaganda films were produced. Some tried to inspire people with the Nazi message; others just promoted hatred

Most newspapers were bought up by Nazi publishers *Eher Verlag*. Papers that printed unpatriotic stories were shut down

The Editors' Law made editors responsible for their papers' content. They were told what to print and only approved journalists could be employed

**Methods of media control**

Loudspeakers were erected in public places and in workplaces

All radio stations were controlled. People were encouraged to buy cheap radios ('People's receivers') which could only pick up Nazi broadcasts

Posters used images and slogans to promote Nazism

## The impact of propaganda and censorship

It is hard to know just how much Germans believed Nazi propaganda.
- Some historians suggest that the Nazi government failed to establish the Nazi *Volksgemeinschaft*.
- It is hard to know just how much Germans believed Nazi propaganda.
- Others have suggested that propaganda was successful when it appealed to existing values including nationalism and **anti-Semitism**.
- The Nazis focused much of their propaganda at young people, seeking to ensure their absolute loyalty.
- Some historians believe that many Germans simply ignored anything which damaged the reputation of the government. That would mean that Nazi propaganda worked, because it persuaded Germans to allow the Nazis to implement their policies.

**What you need to know**

Propaganda was one of Nazis' main methods of control. You should be able to identify the methods used and explain whether or not they worked.

**Revision tasks**

1 Make notes on propaganda under the following headings:
- Meaning
- Person in charge
- Organisations set up
2 Use the following headings to explain Nazi propaganda/**censorship** methods:
- Newspapers
- Radio
- Cinema
- Art
- General

TESTED

Exam practice answers at **www.hoddereducation.co.uk/myrevisionnotesdownloads**

# The extent of support for the Nazis

While the police state limited opposition, not every German supported Hitler. However, while individuals might have complained, there was no organised opposition to the regime until the Second World War. Studies have shown that the Nazis:

- were very popular in rural Protestant areas and among young people
- were popular with the lower middle classes
- had less support from the urban working classes and the unemployed.

In the years 1933–1939, most Germans willingly went along with the regime; some actively believed in Nazi policies and supported them; others supported because they were scared to oppose. The fact that many Germans were imprisoned for political crimes would have had a significant impact on people's attitudes to the regime.

> **What you need to know**
>
> It was important for the Nazis to control all Germans. Make sure you understand the policies introduced and their levels of success.

## Opposition from the churches

Hitler knew that it would be almost impossible to destroy Germany's Churches; however, he wanted to limit their influence. Germany's Churches reacted to the Nazi regime in different ways.

> **What you need to know**
>
> You need to be able to show the examiners that you understand how Germany's different religions responded to the regime.

**Table 1.1 The reaction of Germany's Churches to the Nazi regime**

|  | Catholic Church | Lutheran Church |
|---|---|---|
| Evidence of support | In July 1933, a **concordat** was signed. In return for agreeing not to involve itself in politics, the Catholic Church was allowed to continue running its own schools, services and youth activities. | Pro-Nazi Lutherans – known as German Christians – sought to control all Germany's Protestants. They were led by Bishop Ludwig Müller. |
| Evidence of opposition | By 1936, some of the terms of the concordat were being ignored. In 1937, therefore, Pope Pius XI condemned the regime. | In 1934, Lutherans who opposed Nazism set up the rival Confessional Church. |
| Key individuals | Some Church leaders, such as Bishop Clemens von Galen of Münster, spoke out strongly and successfully against Nazi policies such as **euthanasia**. | A key leader in the Confessional Church was Pastor Martin Niemöller, who was arrested by the Nazis in 1937 and sent to Dachau concentration camp. |

Overall, the Nazis were quite successful in their aim of undermining the influence of Germany's Churches. While a number of individual clerics opposed the regime, by and large the Churches remained more concerned about ensuring their survival.

## Nazi religion

The Nazis created their own Church, the German Faith Movement. Its beliefs owed much more to medieval and **occult** values and to the **Hitler Myth** than to Christianity. It had only around 200,000 followers.

> **Revision tasks**
>
> 1 Create a list of those groups who supported/opposed the Nazis and explain the reasons why.
> 2 Make a table to show the areas of success and the areas of failure for the Nazis' religious policies with reference to the following:
>    - Catholic Church
>    - Lutheran Church
>    - German Faith Movement.
>
> TESTED

# Opposition from young people

While many young Germans loved the **Hitler Youth**, not all supported the regime.

- In 1936, membership of the Hitler Youth became compulsory; up to 1 million young people – some of whom had previously been members of the SDP and KPD youth wings – simply refused to attend.
- Some rebelled by forming their own groups such as **Swing Youth** and the **Edelweiss Pirates**.
- The **Leipzig Hounds** were a **communist** group who listened to Moscow radio.

However, until 1939, few young Germans actively opposed the Nazis.

> **What you need to know**
>
> You must be clear about why young people were so important to the Nazis and understand what the Nazis did to ensure control.

## Exam practice

1 Below is a list of groups/organisations set up by the Nazis:

| Kripo | German Faith Movement | SdA | RAD | BDM |
|---|---|---|---|---|

Match **each** group/organisation to the correct description and write your answer in the space provided. The first one has been done for you.

| | | |
|---|---|---|
| Set up in opposition to Germany's Christian religions | **German Faith Movement** | [1] |
| Set up to undertake public work schemes | | [1] |
| Youth movement for females | | [1] |
| Campaigned to improve working conditions | | [1] |
| Carried out general policing duties | | [1] |

2 Describe two methods used by the Nazis to reduce unemployment. [3+3]

> **Revision task**
>
> Make notes on support and opposition under the following headings:
> - Who supported – and why?
> - Who opposed – and why?
>
> TESTED

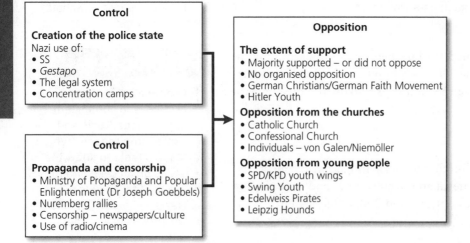

**Summary diagram:** Control and opposition

# 3 Life for workers in Nazi Germany

## Nazi attempts to reduce unemployment

Hitler realised economic recovery was crucial as:

1 the Depression had created hardship and political instability; he needed to create prosperity to stay in power
2 he wanted to go to war; that meant constructing a strong war economy.

In 1934, economist Hjalmar Schacht became Minister of Economics. Schacht's 1934 New Plan oversaw the revitalisation of the economy by:

- introducing massive cuts to welfare spending
- imposing limits on **imports**
- making trade agreements with other countries
- targeting government spending on key industries.

The economy recovered within two years. However, by 1936, Hitler wanted Schacht to increase military spending; unwilling to do this, Schacht resigned.

### The Four-Year Plan

Hermann Göring was appointed to create an economy that was 'ready for war'. In 1936, he introduced the Four-Year Plan. One of its key aims was to ensure that Germany became an **Autarky**.

> **What you need to know**
>
> This is a key area; economic collapse helped Hitler gain power and people expected great change under Nazi rule. You need to know what economic policies were introduced.

Targets were imposed for the production of foodstuffs by the *Reich Food Estate*

Factories were constructed and industries placed under strict government control

The amount of imported goods was cut

The Four-Year Plan

A programme of inventions was started to try to reduce imports

Industries were encouraged to develop artificial substitutes for raw materials

Higher targets were set for the production of essential materials

## Reducing unemployment

The Nazis introduced a number of policies to tackle unemployment:

**Table 1.2** Policies to tackle unemployment

| Area/Group | Action |
| --- | --- |
| Women and Jews | Professional women and Jews were sacked and their jobs were given to the unemployed. Neither group was then counted as unemployed. |
| **Conscription** and rearmament | In 1933, there were 100,000 in the Army. Conscription was introduced in 1935 and by 1939, the Army had 1.4 million members. |
| | As Germany prepared for war, thousands of jobs were created in the armament and associated industries. |
| Public works | The June 1933 Reinhard Programme aimed to build *autobahns*, waterways and railways. A second Programme (September 1933) gave tax incentives for construction projects in rural areas and for house-building in towns. |
| The National Labour Service (RAD) | Established in 1934, the RAD built schools, hospitals and motorways. Six-month membership for all men aged 18–25 became compulsory in 1935. |
| | While no wages were paid, workers received food and a small amount of spending money. Members were removed from the unemployment register. |

## The impact and effectiveness of Nazi actions to reduce unemployment

REVISED

The Nazis had a number of successes in reducing unemployment:

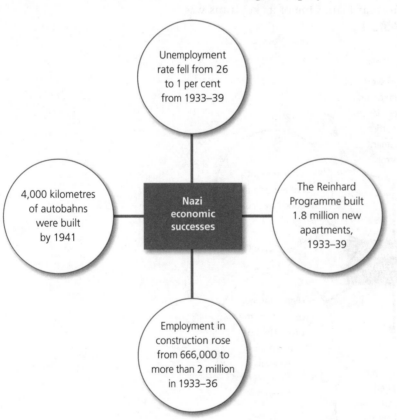

- Unemployment rate fell from 26 to 1 per cent from 1933–39
- 4,000 kilometres of autobahns were built by 1941
- **Nazi economic successes**
- The Reinhard Programme built 1.8 million new apartments, 1933–39
- Employment in construction rose from 666,000 to more than 2 million in 1933–36

> **What you need to know**
>
> Now that you know what policies were introduced to reduce unemployment, examiners will expect you to know just how successful they were.

Despite these, however, the Nazis had a negative effect overall on Germany economy:

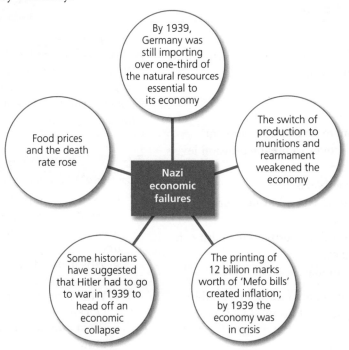

- By 1939, Germany was still importing over one-third of the natural resources essential to its economy
- The switch of production to munitions and rearmament weakened the economy
- Food prices and the death rate rose
- Nazi economic failures
- Some historians have suggested that Hitler had to go to war in 1939 to head off an economic collapse
- The printing of 12 billion marks worth of 'Mefo bills' created inflation; by 1939 the economy was in crisis

**Revision task**

Make notes on Nazi economic policy under the following headings:
- Background
- Aims
- Key personnel
- Policies introduced:
  - Economic recovery
  - Autarchy
  - Unemployment
- Areas of success
- Areas of failure

TESTED ☐

Overall, the Nazis were unsuccessful in their efforts to achieve Autarky. It became clear that the only way to achieve self-sufficiency would be to conquer other countries to gain access to their natural resources.

## Nazi attempts to change the lives of workers

REVISED ☐

Changing the mind-set of Germany's workers was a key aspect of *Volksgemeinschaft*. Three organisations were created to try to accomplish this.

**What you need to know**

Germany's trade unions were powerful; you need to know what Hitler did to destroy their influence – as well as the other steps taken to gain workers' support.

**Table 1.3 Three organisations created to try to change the mind-set of Germany's workers**

| Organisation | Information |
|---|---|
| The German Labour Front (**DAF**) | Hitler was afraid trade unions could interfere with his plans, so in May 1933 they were outlawed. At the same time, striking was declared illegal. |
| | Trade unions were replaced by the DAF. Within two years all workers – more than 20 million people – were members. |
| **The Beauty of Labour (SdA)** | Part of the DAF – the SdA – aimed to encourage workers to be proud of their work. It campaigned to improve conditions through, for example, better lighting, washing facilities or noise reduction. |
| | The Government introduced some health-promotion activities while strongly discouraging heavy drinking. |
| Strength through Joy (**KdF**) | The KdF was established in November 1933 to improve workers' free time and keep them happy outside the workplace. |
| | It provided workers' picnics, cheap cinema and theatre tickets and organised a broad range of sporting activities. Cheap holidays were arranged as a reward for hard work. The flagship KdF scheme was a savings scheme to own a car, the Volkswagen (people's car), by workers contributing five marks each week (until 750 marks had been paid). |

# The impact and effectiveness of Nazi actions on the lives of workers

The DAF was meant to represent the workers in discussions with employers. Instead, it generally sided with employers and workers found their freedoms restricted and their working hours increased.

## Wages and prices

- By 1939, employers' real incomes had increased by 130 per cent.
- Ordinary workers' real wages did not recover to pre-Depression levels until 1938.
- Real wages rose by 20 per cent under the Nazis.
- Working conditions also improved in some ways, but no German ever received a Volkswagen car.
- There were also some improvements in welfare, universal health care, job protection, rent controls and low taxes.
- The Nazis doubled the amount of paid holiday.

However, as money was poured into rearmament, a number of public facilities declined – for instance, in the number of hospital beds and doctors per head of population.

### What you need to know

What you need to know here is simple – did the Nazis' policies relating to workers have an impact?

## Revision tasks

1 Make notes under the following headings about the destruction of trade unions:
- Why it was done
- How it was done
- What it meant for workers
- What it meant for the state

2 Write about the DAF, SdA and KdF under the following headings:
- Purpose
- Leader (if known)
- Tactics
- Reasons it was good for workers
- Reasons it was bad for workers

TESTED

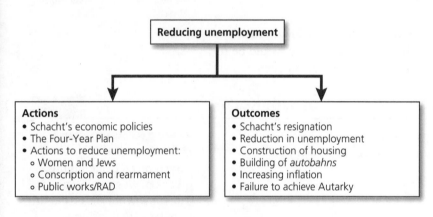

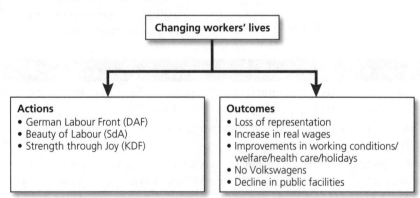

**Summary diagram:** Life for workers in Nazi Germany

# 4 Life for women and the family in Nazi Germany

## Nazi views of women and the family

REVISED

### Aryan ideals

Nazi treatment of women was based on their idea that Germans were descended from a perfect 'Aryan Master Race' which had been 'contaminated' by 'impure blood'. They aimed to re-establish this purity by:
- making Aryan-type women produce as many racially pure children as possible
- stopping 'degenerates' from having children.

> **What you need to know**
>
> You need to explain what role the Nazis saw women having in Germany, how they tried to achieve their aims – and how successful they eventually were.

### Employment

- In Weimar Germany there had been 100,000 female teachers and 3,000 female doctors. Within a year most had been sacked or encouraged to leave.
- From 1933, women could not be appointed to **civil service** positions. In 1936, women were forbidden to become judges.
- The Nazi Women's League was set up to replace women's associations. It was not involved in politics and encouraged its members to be good housekeepers.

### Family life: *Kinder, Küche, Kirche*

- Nazis believed that the family was the foundation unit of the German nation.
- German women also had to meet Nazi social requirements that could be summed up in the phrase 'Children, Kitchen, Church' (*Kinder, Küche, Kirche*) – the 'three Ks'.

### Appearance

Nazi women were expected:
- not to wear makeup, trousers or high heels
- wear their hair arranged in plaits or a bun
- not to smoke.

Slimming was discouraged because it might harm a woman's ability to bear children.

## Nazi actions and policies to change the lives of women and the family

REVISED

### Marriage and babies

The Nazis offered German women incentives to have lots of children.
- The 1933 Law to Reduce Unemployment gave women a 600 mark loan if they married and left work. This loan was reduced for every child born, so couples had children to lessen the debt.
- After 1935, families were given welfare allowances – paid for by increased taxes on the childless.
- After 1938, on days such as Mothering Sunday or the day of Hitler's mother's birthday (12 August), women with four or more children

> **What you need to know**
>
> The Nazis were determined to ensure that Germany's women had lots of children; you need to be able to explain how they tried to achieve this – and how successful they were.

were given an 'Honour Cross'. They were also able to benefit from lower taxation levels and increased state benefits.
- Contraception and abortion became much harder to access.
- SS members were expected to have four children. After 1935, unmarried mothers were encouraged to live in *Lebensborn* homes where SS men could impregnate them.
- Childless couples were encouraged to divorce so that the woman could have the chance of becoming pregnant with someone else. In 1938 such divorces were made easier to obtain.

## Sterilisation and imprisonment

The Nazis only wanted mothers who would have Aryan babies.
- Those who wanted a marriage loan had to get a Certificate of Suitability for Marriage. About one in 25 women failed to get this Certificate due to hereditary illnesses or other 'undesirable' characteristics.
- The Law for the Prevention of Hereditarily Diseased Offspring stated women with hereditary illnesses could be sterilised. By 1939, an estimated 350,000 women had been sterilised.
- After 1938, mothers proposed for an Honour Cross were vetted by the League of Large Families. If it was found that they neglected their children or their housework, they would be 're-educated' and – if they proved unreformable – they were sent to a concentration camp.

## The impact and effectiveness of Nazi policies

REVISED

Nazi rule was a huge set-back for women's rights in Germany; women were simply excluded from public life and leadership. Few women protested and some adopted Nazi values enthusiastically. In 1938, the *NS-Frauenschaft* had 2 million members.
- Evidence suggests that Nazi attempts to increase the birth rate failed.
- It appears that the Certificate of Suitability for Marriage actually discouraged marriage; when the rules were relaxed in 1938, the marriage rate rose.
- The Nazi attempt to exclude women from the workplace also failed. The numbers of women in jobs actually went up in the later 1930s as the drive for rearmament and Autarky took off.
- Faced with a growing skills shortage, after 1937 women had to do a 'Duty Year' in a factory. When the war broke out, women were needed to help the war effort.

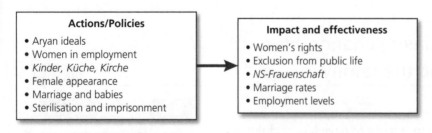

| Actions/Policies | Impact and effectiveness |
|---|---|
| • Aryan ideals<br>• Women in employment<br>• *Kinder, Küche, Kirche*<br>• Female appearance<br>• Marriage and babies<br>• Sterilisation and imprisonment | • Women's rights<br>• Exclusion from public life<br>• *NS-Frauenschaft*<br>• Marriage rates<br>• Employment levels |

**Summary diagram: Life for women and the family in Nazi Germany**

### Revision tasks

1 Explain what role the Nazis saw women having in their regime.
2 Create a spider diagram showing the different strategies used by the Nazis towards women in terms of employment, family life and appearance.
3 Create another spider diagram to explain the actions taken by the Nazis to encourage German women to have children.

TESTED

### What you need to know

You need to explain how effective the Nazis' policies were in terms of women, births and their role in Germany.

### Revision tasks

1 Explain what the Nazis' policies were in relation to marriage and sterilisation.
2 Create a spider diagram showing the impact and effectiveness of Nazi policies towards women.

TESTED

# 5 Life for young people in Nazi Germany

## Nazi actions and policies to change the lives of young people

REVISED

The Nazis saw the indoctrination of youth with Nazi ideas as the key to their control of the country. Boys were Germany's future military and political leaders; girls were the country's future mothers. So they set about influencing children inside and outside school.

> **What you need to know**
>
> You need to be clear about why young people were so important to the Nazis and also make sure you can explain what they did to ensure control outside school.

## Youth movements

REVISED

**Table 1.4 Nazi youth groups for boys and girls**

| Age | Boys | Girls |
|-----|------|-------|
| 6–10 | Cubs (*Pimpfe*) | |
| 10–14 | Young German Folk (*Deutsches Jungvolk*) | Young Maidens (*Jung Mädel*) |
| 14–18 | Hitler Youth (*Hitlerjugend*) | League of German Maidens (*Bund Deutscher Mädel*) |
| 18–21 | | Faith and Beauty (*Glaube und Schönheit*) |

> **What you need to know**
>
> There are a number of different Nazi youth groups; be clear about the purpose of each.

### The Hitler Youth (*Hitlerjugend* – HJ)

The HJ was led by Baldur von Schirach. It was organised into different sections (see Table 1.4) and had two main aims:

- to indoctrinate racism
- to develop physical fitness in Germany's youths.

A 1936 Youth Law made the HJ all but compulsory. The Boy Scouts movement was banned and pressure was put on Catholic Youth Clubs to disband. Upon joining the HJ, a boy would be put on probation, during which time he had to:

- learn about the HJ and Hitler
- learn the words of the *Horst Wessel* song
- run 60 metres, go on a hike and complete a 'courage test'.

HJ members received a monthly magazine called *Will and Power* and took part in lots of exciting activities.

By 1938, the HJ had over 7 million members. After war broke out, all boys were automatically conscripted into the HJ, which was reformed into the '**home guard**' force. In 1945, with Germany's army destroyed and the USSR advancing, Goebbels organised a German Home Defence Force made up of HJ members and old men, for a last–ditch defence of Berlin.

## The League of German Maidens (*Bund Deutscher Mädel* or BDM)

Led by Trude Mohr, the BDM was the girls' version of the HJ; it was also organised into age groups. It aimed to teach German girls how to keep themselves fit for childbirth and be good mothers.

BDM members received a monthly magazine called *Maiden's Works* and took part in lots of activities.

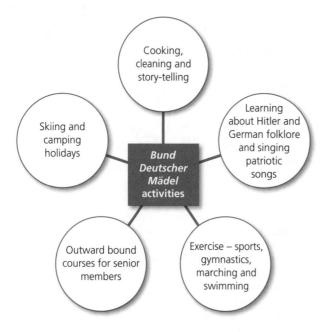

The idea that a good Nazi woman put others and the nation first ran through everything the BDM did. After 1943, many BDM girls went into 'home guard' service, though rarely to fight.

## Revision tasks

1 Why were young people so important to the Nazis?
2 Create a spider diagram that shows the different youth groups set up by the Nazis.
3 How did the activities of Nazi youth groups for boys and girls differ? Why was this?

TESTED

# Education

The Nazis sought to train Germany's youth to accept that they should be ready to sacrifice themselves for Germany and Hitler. Therefore, the government:

- dismissed Jewish and 'unreliable' teachers
- encouraged teachers to join the National Socialist Teachers' League (NSLB) and to promote Nazism at all times. Within six years 97 per cent of teachers had joined
- sent primary school teachers to special training camps
- asked HJ and BDM members to report teachers who were not 'Nazi' enough.

> **What you need to know**
>
> The Nazis also used school to gain and maintain control over Germany's youth. Make sure you understand what they did and how successful they were.

## The Nazi curriculum

The curriculum was also Nazified.

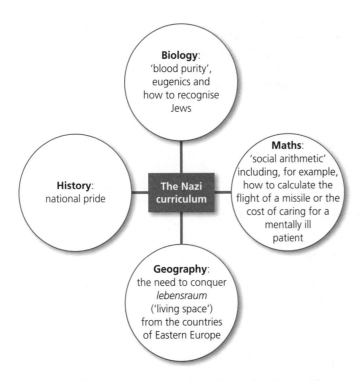

**The Nazi curriculum**

**Biology**: 'blood purity', eugenics and how to recognise Jews

**History**: national pride

**Maths**: 'social arithmetic' including, for example, how to calculate the flight of a missile or the cost of caring for a mentally ill patient

**Geography**: the need to conquer *lebensraum* ('living space') from the countries of Eastern Europe

Girls followed a different curriculum, which taught them to be good wives and mothers – cookery, needlework, housekeeping and PE.

## Nazi special schools

Special schools were set up for young men whom the Nazis hoped would form the Nazi elite of the future.

- Boys aged 11–18 could be sent to the National Political Institutes of Education – where they were trained to be soldiers.
- In Adolf Hitler Schools, four-fifths of the curriculum was given over to PE and boys were also taught German 'folklore'.
- Order Castles were the elite schools. There, students were brutally prepared to be SS officers, and subjects included war games with live ammunition.

# The impact and effectiveness of Nazi actions and policies by 1939

Nazi youth policies had mixed results. Most young people accepted them unquestioningly and would have been influenced by the Nazi policies both inside and outside the classroom.

**What you need to know**

What you need to know here is simple – were Nazi policies in this area successful, or not?

**Table 1.5 Arguments for and against Nazi youth policies**

| Arguments 'for' | Arguments 'against' |
|---|---|
| • Some members of the Hitler Youth loved the movements and their exciting activities and marches.<br>• The Nazis achieved their aim of brainwashing young people. In 1936, on Hitler's birthday, thousands of Hitler Youth members promised loyalty unto death to Hitler. In 1945, they fought and died for him.<br>• The Patrol Force, part of the Hitler Youth, successfully informed on opponents. Adults were scared of what members might tell the authorities; this gave young people a power they enjoyed. | • Evidence suggests that the quality and breadth of education suffered badly.<br>• Students' education was harmed by their continual absences to attend the Hitler Youth and BDM.<br>• As many as 1 million youths avoided joining the Nazi youth movements and even established rival youth groups of their own. |

## Exam practice

3 Below are the names of two religious leaders who opposed the Nazis during the period 1939–45.

Choose one individual and explain how he opposed Nazi rule. [6]

Martin Niemöller        Clemens von Galen

4 How did Nazi policies impact on the lives of women in Germany in the years 1933–39? [8]

**Youth groups – Boys**
• Cubs
• Young German Folk
• Hitler Youth:
  ○ Led by Baldur von Schirach
  ○ To indoctrinate and train
  ○ Variety of activities
  ○ Changing role during the Second World War

**Youth groups – Girls**
• Young Maidens
• League of German Maidens:
  ○ Girls' version of the Hitler Youth
  ○ How to be good mothers
  ○ How to keep fit
• Faith and beauty

**Impact and effectiveness**
• Support for youth movements
• Success of indoctrination
• Role of young people as informers
• Reduction in quality of education
• Impact of attendance at youth movements on student learning
• Existence of rival youth groups

**Summary diagram:** Life for young people in Nazi Germany

Exam practice answers at **www.hoddereducation.co.uk/myrevisionnotesdownloads**

# 6 Life for the Jewish community and minorities in Nazi Germany

## The persecution of minorities

REVISED

In the early twentieth century, some believed that some races were superior to others. Most Germans believed that they were descended from an Aryan 'Master Race'.

### Nazi racial ideas and policies

**Table 1.6 Races the Nazis considered to be 'good' or 'inferior'**

| 'Good' races | 'Inferior' races |
|---|---|
| The English and Danes – even the French – had some Germanic blood in them. | The Slav races were fit only to be slaves. Many black Germans were sterilised or killed. |

The Nazis also believed that marriage or relationships between people of different races would 'pollute' German blood. The Nazis concluded that many people were simply *Untermenschen* (sub-human).

Many scientists believed that the answer to this was 'eugenics' (good genes). This is why the Nazis:
- encouraged Aryan-type mothers to have as many children as possible
- recommended sterilisation of the 'unfit'
- considered a whole range of races and groups *Untermenschen*, whom they believed had to be eliminated from the gene pool.

## The treatment of minorities

REVISED

Prisoners in concentration camps were forced to wear a coloured triangle representing their 'crime'.
- '**Asocial**' Germans – included the 'work shy', vagrants, alcoholics, prostitutes and pacifists. Although not guilty of any crime, thousands were sent to concentration camps, where many died.
- Those with mental and physical disabilities and illnesses. The Diseased Offspring Law of 1933 allowed sterilisation of the disabled and, after 1935, doctors were allowed to terminate pregnancies by force. In 1939–41, the Nazis conducted a programme of euthanasia.
- The Roma ('Gypsies'), whom the Nazis also saw as a great a danger to Aryan blood purity. The Roma holocaust is called the *Porajmos* ('cutting up'); perhaps a third of the estimated 700,000 Roma people in Europe were killed.
- Homosexual men. 100,000 homosexual men were arrested; 15,000 were sent to concentration camps. Some were castrated; others were experimented on to try to find a 'cure'. The Nazis **forbade** lesbianism, but classified it as 'asocial' rather than a criminal act.
- Jehovah's Witnesses. There were about 25,000 in Germany. Their religion was banned and they were placed in prison or put into mental institutions. Some 2,000 were sent to concentration camps and 250 were executed.
- Political opponents were sent to concentration camps. Many political prisoners were students and intellectuals; many died.
- 'Career criminals' were sent to labour camps. Ordinary criminals were imprisoned.

> **What you need to know**
>
> Nazi policy towards the Jews is a crucial element for you to understand. You should also be fully aware of how they dealt with other 'inferior' groups.

> **What you need to know**
>
> While we rightly remember the Nazis' unspeakable treatment of Jews, they also dealt severely with many other individuals/groups. Many of these ended up in concentration camps.

> **Revision tasks**
>
> 1  List three key points about Nazi racial ideas/policies.
> 2  Create a table – with the headings Group/Actions/Outcomes – that shows the key elements of the Nazis' policy towards different minority groups.
>
> TESTED

# Nazi persecution of the Jewish community

The Nazis reserved their greatest hatred for Germany's Jews; they argued that Jews were to blame for many of Germany's problems. Once in power, Hitler aimed to isolate them and remove their influence.

**What you need to know**

You must be able to explain how Nazi policy towards Jews changed and developed.

**Table 1.7** Actions taken to isolate the Jews from German society

| Date | Action taken |
|---|---|
| April 1933 | Jews banned from government jobs. |
| September 1935 | Nuremberg Laws:<br>● Jews deprived of many political and economic rights (*Reich* Citizenship Law).<br>● Illegal for Jews and Aryans to marry or engage in sexual relations outside marriage (Law for the Protection of German Blood and German Honour). |
| January 1937 | Jews banned from key professions – including teaching, accountancy and dentistry. |
| July/August 1938 | Jews had to carry identity cards. |
| October 1938 | Jews to have their passports stamped with a J-shaped symbol and forced to use new names: Israel for men, Sarah for women. |
| November 1938 | The murder of a Nazi diplomat by a Jew in Paris led to a massive outbreak of anti-Jewish persecution, known as *Kristallnacht*. |

# The impact and effectiveness of Nazi actions and policies by 1939

By 1939 the Nazis' actions against Germany's Jews had had a significant impact. The nature and quality of Jews' lives had been damaged – the Jews were constrained, isolated and oppressed.

● Jewish Germans' self-esteem (which would affect their response when the Nazis started their genocide) had been reduced. Many Jews (including the scientist Albert Einstein) fled Germany.

● Their role in German life had been successfully strangled by Nazi policies.

The Nazis' actions against the Jews were not opposed by many ordinary Germans. A combination of support, education, ignorance or fear ensured that persecution of the Jews was able to go ahead.

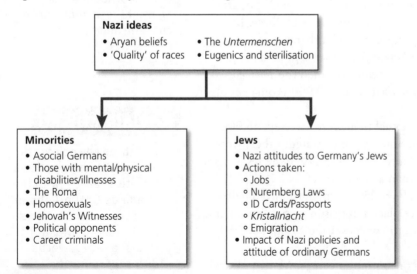

**Nazi ideas**
● Aryan beliefs
● 'Quality' of races
● The *Untermenschen*
● Eugenics and sterilisation

**Minorities**
● Asocial Germans
● Those with mental/physical disabilities/illnesses
● The Roma
● Homosexuals
● Jehovah's Witnesses
● Political opponents
● Career criminals

**Jews**
● Nazi attitudes to Germany's Jews
● Actions taken:
  ○ Jobs
  ○ Nuremberg Laws
  ○ ID Cards/Passports
  ○ *Kristallnacht*
  ○ Emigration
● Impact of Nazi policies and attitude of ordinary Germans

**Summary diagram:** Life for the Jewish community and minorities in Nazi Germany

**Revision tasks**

1 Create a spider diagram that illustrates the key elements/developments in the Nazis' treatment of Germany's Jews (1933–1939).

2 How successful were the Nazis' actions against Germany's Jewish population before the War? Why was this?

TESTED

# 7 Germany at war

## The impact of the war on the German people

REVISED

At first the war had a relatively limited impact. Early military successes helped increase Hitler's popularity, while Germans experienced few shortages.

However, the population did feel some negative effects of the war.
- Some rationing was introduced at the start of the war. From November 1939, clothes and footwear were rationed, as was soap – even though Germans were only allowed to use hot water two days a week.
- Fearing RAF bombing, in September 1940 the evacuation of children from Berlin was ordered. In the end, this bombing did not begin until 1942.

### The role of propaganda

As the war went on and successes dwindled, the role of propaganda increased. Following defeats at Stalingrad (February 1943) and **Allied** bombing raids, Goebbels urged Germans to make even greater sacrifices to achieve ultimate victory.

### Air raids and bombing

From 1942, Germans began to experience the devastation of Allied bombing raids. The Allies wanted to destroy Germans' spirit and thus force an early end to the war.

A number of key German cities came under attack:
- Cologne, on 30 May 1942
- Hamburg, on two main occasions – July and August 1943; thousands died and the majority of buildings were destroyed
- Dresden, in February 1945; nearly three-quarters of its buildings were destroyed while 150,000 civilians were killed.

By the time that the European war ended (May 1945), it is estimated that at least 3.5 million civilians had lost their lives. Some historians argue that the raids helped unite Germany, but there is also evidence that popular disaffection was growing, particularly after defeat at Stalingrad.

> **What you need to know**
>
> While we often focus on battles when studying wars, it is equally important to understand the impact that the Second World War had on ordinary Germans.

Option 1 Life under Nazi dictatorship, 1933–45

# Total War and rationing

Total War was first declared by Goebbels in February 1943. By then it was clear that Germany was not winning the war and did not have an economy suited to the kind of war now being fought. Total War meant that all economic activity would be focused on the task of winning the war.

**What you need to know**

It is important that you understand the meaning of these terms and the impact that their introduction had.

## Total War

- Fritz Todt was tasked with reorganising the economy to this end.
- Albert Speer became Minister for Armaments and Production after Todt's death (February 1942). He ensured that all factories focused on production to support the war effort.
- Speer's mass production techniques ensured that industrial productivity increased.

## Rationing

The failure to defeat the USSR in 1942 meant that rationing had to be increased, while artificial substitutes had to be found for scarce goods.

As a consequence:
- many Germans experienced real hunger
- public parks and private gardens were used to grow vegetables
- people were encouraged to try new recipes and to eat a one-dish meal on Sundays
- many shops displayed make-believe produce
- in 1943, the production of non-military clothing stopped and Exchange Centres were set up to enable people to swap clothing and household items. These shortages led to the emergence of a **black market**
- additional rations were made available to those working in heavy industries, while pregnant women and blood donors received extra supplies. However, by 1945 there were real shortages of clothing and food. That said, the rationing of foodstuffs meant that for a time Germans were eating a more balanced diet.

## Labour shortages and the role of women in the workplace

Even before the war, the increasing number of men being conscripted meant that there were over 6 million women at work.

Many women, however, were unwilling to join the workforce. Therefore:
- in January 1943, the government had to conscript women to work
- by 1944, more than 40 per cent of women were working, making up more than half of the workforce.

However, this was not enough and so the regime was also forced to use foreign workers and prisoners of war. Many more were employed as compulsory labourers in the countries occupied by the Nazis.

**Revision tasks**

1 Create a spider diagram showing the impact that the war had on ordinary Germans.
2 Create a table – with the headings Definition/Key Leaders/Impact – that shows the key elements of Total War.
3 How successful was the Nazis' policy of Total War? Why was this?

TESTED

# Escalation of racial persecution

Until 1941, German Jews had the option of emigration – overseen by the *Reich* Central Office for Jewish Emigration. It is estimated that as many as half of Germany's Jewish population left in this manner before 1939.
- The decision to ban such emigration in 1941 meant that one route of escape was closed off.
- As Germany's army moved into Eastern Europe, it is estimated that over 3 million additional Jews came under Nazi control.
- As a result, the Nazis decided that new methods would be needed to deal with the Jewish issue.
- In Summer 1940, the government's 'Jewish Department' suggested exiling all Europe's Jews to Madagascar; this proved impossible as the Royal Navy was blockading German ports.

> **What you need to know**
>
> The Nazis' determination to persecute minorities grew with the outbreak of war. You need to understand the actions taken – as well as their horrific outcome.

## The *Einsatzgruppen* and Ghettos

Between 1939 and 1942, SS *Einsatzgruppen* squads rounded up Jews in the newly-occupied territories and executed them in their thousands. Historians estimate that by 1943, 2 million people, mainly Jews, had been murdered in this way.

Many of the Jews living in Polish cities found themselves living in Ghettos after the start of the war.
- At first the Ghettos were 'open', but later they were 'sealed'. Anybody trying to leave was shot.
- The Nazis created at least 1,000 Ghettos, each with a Jewish Council nominally in control. The Nazis used Ghetto Jews as forced labour.
- The largest Ghetto was in Warsaw. Living conditions were harsh and dirty and many people died of disease (such as typhus). The Nazis imposed starvation rations, so thousands starved or froze to death.

## The Final Solution

The increasing number of Jews under Nazi control meant that new methods of elimination had to be found.
- On 20 January 1942 senior Nazis met in Wannsee to decide how to deal with the 'Jewish Problem'.
- They decided to establish Death Camps to execute Europe's Jews.
- This decision became known as the Final Solution.

> **What you need to know**
>
> Examiners will expect you to be able to explain what the Final Solution was and how it worked in practice.

## The Death Camps

- A number of camps were built in occupied Eastern Europe. The most infamous was Auschwitz-Birkenau, in southern Poland.
- Upon arrival, the Nazis confiscated the Jews' possessions. Then those deemed unfit for work were sent to the gas chambers where they were executed using Zyklon B (hydrogen cyanide). At Treblinka, Sobibor, Belzec and Chelmno, prisoners were killed in the gas chambers by exhaust fumes. *Sonderkommando* units then extracted any gold teeth from the dead and burned their bodies.
- Those deemed fit for work were used for forced labour. When unable to work any longer, they were sent to the gas chambers.
- By the time the war in Europe ended (May 1945), an estimated 6 million Jews had been murdered. Similar strategies were also used against the Roma.

> **Revision task**
>
> Create a timeline showing the development of racial persecution/the Final Solution.
>
> TESTED

# Growing opposition and resistance in Germany, 1939–45

REVISED

The majority of Germans remained loyal to the regime during the war; however, opposition did emerge from the Kreisau Circle and the Beck–Goerdeler Group. While there was also opposition from the communist Red Orchestra, the most effective opposition came from youth groups, the Churches and from within the military.

### What you need to know

While opposition was limited, some Germans did try to oppose the regime. You need to be able to explain who these opponents were, why they opposed, what actions they took and what the outcomes were.

## Youth groups

REVISED

Three main youth groups showed their opposition to the Nazis.

**Table 1.8 The three main youth groups that showed opposition to the Nazis**

| Group | Details |
|-------|---------|
| Swing Youth | • Swing Youth membership came mostly from the upper and middle classes and was largely urban-based.<br>• Members were not particularly political but enjoyed listening to jazz music and attending bars and clubs.<br>• The Nazis closed down such locations. |
| Edelweiss Pirates | • Edelweiss Pirates were generally from a working-class background.<br>• They had refused to join the Hitler Youth; instead they spent their time mocking and beating up that group's members.<br>• During the war, they distributed propaganda leaflets dropped by Allied aircraft. |
| The White Rose | • The non-violent White Rose movement was set up in 1942 by Munich University undergraduates Hans and Sophie Scholl.<br>• The distribution of anti-Nazi leaflets was one of the activities undertaken by the group, which also appealed to Germans not to support the war effort.<br>• The main members were executed by the *Gestapo*. |

## The Churches

REVISED

While Germany's main Churches did not speak out against the Nazis, individual religious leaders did oppose the regime.

**Table 1.9 Religious leaders who opposed the Nazi regime**

| Church | Details |
|--------|---------|
| Confessional Church | • Lutheran pastors such as Dietrich Bonhoeffer and Martin Niemöller opposed the National *Reich* Church and established the Confessional Church.<br>• Bonhoeffer became more politically involved and participated in anti-Nazi activities; he was executed in April 1945.<br>• Niemöller also ended up imprisoned in concentration camps; he survived. |
| Catholic Church | • Some priests opposed Hitler; many hid Jews during the holocaust and thousands were sent to concentration camps.<br>• The Bishop of Münster, Clemens von Galen, spoke out against the regime, preaching particularly against its use of euthanasia. As a result, the Nazis were forced to abandon the policy.<br>• Von Galen also spoke out against forced sterilisation, concentration camps and the activities of the *Gestapo*. |

Exam practice answers at **www.hoddereducation.co.uk/myrevisionnotesdownloads**

# Jewish reactions to the Nazis

There is plenty of evidence that Jews did not simply accept their persecution.

## Armed resistance

- In April–May 1943, Jews in the Warsaw Ghetto killed 300 Germans; 13,000 Jews died. There were dozens of other Ghetto rebellions.
- Many Jews fought in resistance groups. In eastern Poland, 1941–44, the Bielski brothers led a Jewish resistance group which attacked Nazis and helped more than 1,200 Jews to escape.
- There was resistance in the death camps. At Treblinka and Sobibor, Jews attacked guards and organised mass escapes. In Auschwitz, the *Sonderkommando* stole some explosives and blew up a crematorium.

## Emigration and hiding

Jews also tried to avoid the holocaust. More than half of Germany's and Austria's Jews managed to emigrate or flee. Some 15,000 German children were sent out of Germany unaccompanied. Many Jews went to Palestine; others hid.

## Non-violent resistance

Other Jews worked to undermine the Nazis. In the Ghettos they smuggled food, produced underground newspapers, forged papers and destroyed files.

## Co-operation

Sometimes, even Jews who seemed to be co-operating with the Nazis were actually working against them. Everywhere they conquered, Nazis set up 'Jewish Councils' to help them run the Ghettos. Though denounced as collaborators, many were trying to reduce the suffering by co-operating. In Holland, the Jewish Council organised deportations to the death camps – but arranged 15,000 exemptions and made sure there were endless delays and no brutality.

# The Army

The most serious attempt to remove Hitler came from the Army. Although some senior officers were not fans of the *Führer*, it was difficult to oppose him while the war was going well. By 1943, however, the war was going badly; as a result, opposition grew.

## Operation Valkyrie

In 1944, some opponents agreed to assassinate Hitler. They were led by General Ludwig Beck and Dr Carl Goerdeler. The assassination was to be carried out by Colonel Claus von Stauffenberg. Known as Operation Valkyrie, the plot developed as follows:

- Von Stauffenberg was to leave a bomb in Hitler's Wolf's Lair. After the bomb had exploded, the plot leaders would seize control of Berlin.
- Initial attempts to plant the bomb failed; on 17 July, Hitler ordered the arrest of Dr Goerdeler – who managed to evade capture.
- On 20 July, von Stauffenberg placed the bomb and returned to Berlin. However, someone moved the case containing the bomb. When it exploded, four people were killed; however, Hitler survived.

- The plotters' failure to gain swift control of Berlin meant that by the same evening the plot had failed.
- Following the failure of the plot, thousands were executed; many others committed suicide.
- In the plot's aftermath, all members of the Army had again to swear an Oath of Loyalty to Hitler.

## The effectiveness of opposition and resistance up to 1945

Judging the success of opposition is relatively straightforward – no German-based group or citizen was able to stop or defeat Hitler. Fear of the regime played a significant part in ensuring conformity. At the same time, the destruction of the party system and the weakening of trade unions robbed Germans of a means of demonstrating their opposition. Despite some domestic opposition, the regime was able to continue until its ultimate defeat in 1945.

At the same time, the determination of some groups and individuals to express their opposition to the regime was proof of Hitler's failure to gain control over every German and not every Nazi policy was implemented successfully.

## Revision tasks

1 Create a spider diagram showing the different groups that opposed the Nazis during the war.
2 Create a table – with the headings Group/Actions/Impact – that explains who opposed, what methods they used and how successful they were in their opposition.

TESTED ☐

## Exam practice

5 'The main opposition to the Nazis in the years 1939–45 came from the German Army.'

Do you agree? Explain your answer. [16]

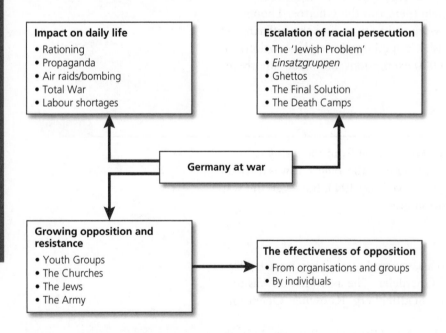

**Impact on daily life**
- Rationing
- Propaganda
- Air raids/bombing
- Total War
- Labour shortages

**Escalation of racial persecution**
- The 'Jewish Problem'
- *Einsatzgruppen*
- Ghettos
- The Final Solution
- The Death Camps

**Germany at war**

**Growing opposition and resistance**
- Youth Groups
- The Churches
- The Jews
- The Army

**The effectiveness of opposition**
- From organisations and groups
- By individuals

**Summary diagram:** Germany at war

# Option 2 Life in the United States of America, 1920–33

## 1 Life for minority groups

### Problems faced by black Americans in the southern states

REVISED

The **Jim Crow** laws were passed in the former slave-owning states of the south to restrict the rights of former slaves.

#### Jim Crow laws and civil rights

These laws meant that black people could not:
- attend white schools
- sit in the white carriages on trains
- go to white libraries, restaurants, cinemas, churches and swimming pools.

In 1896, the **Plessy v. Ferguson** case said black people had to be 'separate but equal' which made **segregation** legal.

Until 1954, black Americans were second-class citizens. They:
- could not vote or sit on juries, could not influence legal decisions
- were convicted of crimes even when evidence showed they were innocent
- were forbidden to marry white people by the anti-**miscegenation** laws
- became **sharecroppers**.

#### The rise of the Ku Klux Klan (KKK)

Black Americans who challenged white supremacy risked being **lynched**.
- 1,360 black Americans were lynched between 1900–19, 281 in the 1920s and 119 in the 1930s.
- When some black Americans tried to prevent a lynching in Tulsa, Oklahoma, in 1921, a white mob raided the black neighbourhoods, burning 1,256 homes and killing 26 black Americans.

A former church-minister called William J Simmons re-established the Ku Klux Klan – a right-wing extremist group which wanted to 'purify' American society.

#### The actions of the KKK

The Klan wore a uniform of long white robes and carried out many of their activities in secret. They attacked anyone who did not match their white, Anglo-Saxon, Protestant (WASP) definition of being American. This included Catholics, Jews, Communists, homosexuals, divorcees and, particularly, black Americans.

Membership rose to almost 5 million and, in August 1925, 50,000 Klansmen marched through Washington to show their popularity. When caught and brought to trial, Klansmen found themselves in front of police, judges and juries who were Klansmen too, and were let off.

> **What you need to know**
>
> You need to be able to explain how the lives of black Americans were affected by the resentment and racism of white Americans.

> **Revision task**
>
> Explain how each of the following problems affected the lives of black Americans:
> - the Jim Crow laws
> - segregation
> - lynching
> - the Ku Klux Klan.
>
> TESTED

## Black Americans in the northern states

During the First World War, half a million black Americans moved north for better wages, job opportunities and escape from the racial oppression they faced in the south. 800,000 black Americans left the south in the 1920s and 400,000 more in the 1930s. This was called 'the Great Migration'.

Black men worked in dangerous industries such as steel, automotive and meatpacking; female workers became maids. The number of black people living in New York increased by 66 per cent and in Detroit by 600 per cent.

## Racism and riots

More workers caused wages to fall and rents to rise, which angered local poor white workers. There were race riots in a number of northern towns in 1919 – 38 people were killed in Chicago.

Black people crowded into areas of poor housing called 'ghettos', creating a racial divide in northern towns when black families moved into areas, while white families moved out.

Trade unions had a 'whites-only' policy. Black Americans were the last to be hired and the first to be fired.

Black Americans in the north looked down on the poorly-educated people from the south.

## Political and cultural responses of black Americans

Faced by legal, political and economic discrimination, black Americans began to take action to achieve equality.

# Problems faced by immigrants

America was seen as the 'land of opportunity' and freedom. In the early nineteenth century, immigrants came from western and northern Europe, but by the end of the century there were more immigrants from eastern Europe, Asia and Mexico.

## Attitudes towards immigration

Although almost all Americans were originally from immigrant families, there were several reasons for a generally hostile attitude to immigration in the 1920s.

**What you need to know**

You need to be able to explain how the USA's policy towards immigration changed from allowing and encouraging it, to fearing and restricting it.

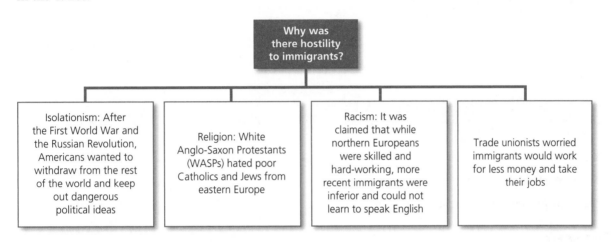

**Why was there hostility to immigrants?**

- Isolationism: After the First World War and the Russian Revolution, Americans wanted to withdraw from the rest of the world and keep out dangerous political ideas
- Religion: White Anglo-Saxon Protestants (WASPs) hated poor Catholics and Jews from eastern Europe
- Racism: It was claimed that while northern Europeans were skilled and hard-working, more recent immigrants were inferior and could not learn to speak English
- Trade unionists worried immigrants would work for less money and take their jobs

## Restrictions on immigration in the 1920s

By the 1920s, the US government wanted to limit immigration by discouraging 'undesirable' people. The laws they passed (see diagram on the next page) tried to restrict immigration to the white, northern European countries.

Meanwhile, the **Federal** Bureau of Naturalization organised courses on democracy to prepare immigrants for a 'citizenship exam', to get them to become 'true Americans'.

## Impact on the lives of immigrants

In the 1920s, immigrants lived in overcrowded slums alongside other immigrants from their own country. For example, in New York:
- The Lower East Side (the Jewish community)
- 'Little Italy'
- 'Chinatown'.

They worked long hours in poorly-paid manual jobs. Immigrants kept to themselves. Living in poverty meant that many became ill, or took to drunkenness and gambling.

## Revision tasks

TESTED

1. Explain why there was hostility towards immigrants in the USA.
2. Make notes on the ways in which the US government restricted immigration.
3. People called the USA the 'land of opportunity' for immigrants. How accurate do you think this description was in the 1920s? Explain your answer.

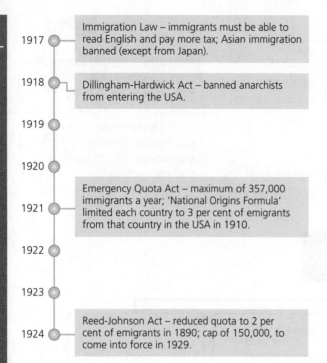

1917 — Immigration Law – immigrants must be able to read English and pay more tax; Asian immigration banned (except from Japan).

1918 — Dillingham-Hardwick Act – banned anarchists from entering the USA.

1919

1920

1921 — Emergency Quota Act – maximum of 357,000 immigrants a year; 'National Origins Formula' limited each country to 3 per cent of emigrants from that country in the USA in 1910.

1922

1923

1924 — Reed-Johnson Act – reduced quota to 2 per cent of emigrants in 1890; cap of 150,000, to come into force in 1929.

## Revision task

Make a list of all of the problems that immigrants into the USA faced. How would you explain why they were prepared to face these problems?

TESTED

## Hostility towards immigrants

In the 1920s, immigrants were treated with suspicion.

### The Red Scare

The 1917 **Russian Revolution** frightened Americans into thinking communists would bring **atheism** and violence to the USA. The US government passed the Sedition Act in 1918, making it illegal to criticise or abuse the US government, flag or army.

### The Palmer Raids

In 1919, mail bombs were sent to US politicians; and other bombs exploded in US cities. There were also lots of strikes which were blamed on communists. The US Attorney-General, Mitchell Palmer, had his house bombed. He told Congress that **radicals** were planning to destroy the government.

Palmer arrested thousands of suspects. Most were members of the Communist Party, although some were trade unionists, Jews, Catholics or black Americans. There was opposition to this from many high-level officials and judges and so the raids stopped. Most immigrants were released; some were deported.

### The Sacco and Vanzetti case

In 1920, two Italian **anarchists**, Nicola Sacco and Bartolomeo Vanzetti, were accused of killing two guards during a robbery. At their trial in 1921 they both had strong alibis, but were found guilty. The jury did not believe them. Even when a different criminal confessed to the murders in 1925, the courts refused to believe him.

Sacco and Vanzetti appealed to the courts to let them go, but failed. They were executed in August 1927.

# Problems faced by Native Americans

## Background

As the United States expanded west, white settlers wanted to use the Native American land for railroads, mining and building dams. They believed in **manifest destiny** – that God wanted them to civilise the 'primitive' Native Americans.

## The Native American way of life

After 1867, Native Americans had to live on **reservations**. This was meant to destroy their way of life. Because of racism, they were not allowed the same rights as other US citizens and were expected to live like white famers. They were promised supplies and medicines.

## The policy of 'allotment'

The **Bureau of Indian Affairs** gave white Americans the right to develop Native American land. The Dawes Act of 1887, divided Native American reservations into 'allotments'. They were given to individual Native Americans. Native Americans found that they could not make money from their land and had to sell it. By the end of the 1920s, two-thirds of tribal lands had been sold to white settlers.

## The impact on Native Americans

The Meriam Report, a privately funded study into the lives of Native Americans in the 1920s, in 1928 found that on average Native Americans earned a sixth as much as white Americans. This resulted in poor health, malnutrition and a high infant mortality rate. It said the land that had been given to the Native Americans was unsuitable for farming.

## The experience of Native Americans

Native American religious practices were forbidden in many states. In 1903, the **US Supreme Court** declared that Native Americans were 'wards of the nation'. This gave the government rights over the Native American lands, culture, language, religion, art and education.

White Americans believed that Native Americans should be **assimilated** into white American culture.

> ### What you need to know
>
> You need to be able to explain how racist attitudes threatened the traditional culture and lifestyle of Native Americans.

> ### Revision task
> TESTED
>
> Make a list of the ways the US government tried to control Native Americans. Which is the most important? Explain your choice.

## The education of Native Americans

The Bureau of Indian Affairs set up boarding schools for young Native Americans. Children were given European-style haircuts and uniforms and new English-sounding names. They had to go to Christian church services and were not allowed to speak their own languages.

Native American parents were bullied by the government into sending their children to the schools. The Meriam Report recommended that Native American students should be taught their own culture and that there should be more schools on the reservations.

## Changing attitudes towards Native Americans in the USA

As the public became more aware of how Native Americans were treated, things began to improve.

1911    The Society of American Indians published the American Indian Magazine and campaigned for an 'American Indian Day'.

1923    The Indian Defense Association argued that Native American culture was superior to American society.

1924    The Snyder Act gave Native Americans full US citizenship rights.

1928    The Meriam Report highlighted the how the US government had mistreated Native Americans.

1933    Roosevelt's 'New Deal' included an Indian Civilian Conservation Corps, an Indian Emergency Conservation Work program and an Indian Arts and Crafts Board.

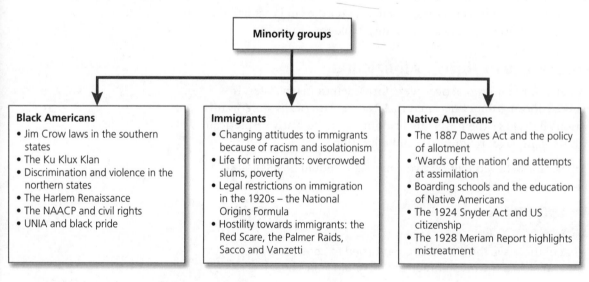

**Summary diagram:** Life for minority groups

# 2 Prohibition

## The introduction of Prohibition

REVISED

Congress passed the 18th **Amendment** in 1919. It banned making, selling and transporting alcohol in America. Prohibition Agents tried to stop illegal selling of alcohol.

### Reasons for and aims of Prohibition

**Temperance** organisations argued that alcohol destroyed families and caused accidents. They wanted people to stop drinking it. They were supported by religious groups, women's groups, doctors and even the Ku Klux Klan.

During the First World War, the government had already reduced alcohol consumption so that workers could concentrate on their work. It was a popular idea.

### The growth and impact of organised crime

Some people made their own 'moonshine' (illegal alcohol), others visited 'speakeasies' (illegal bars). Prohibition Agents could not stop 'bootleggers' smuggling alcohol.

Criminals organised **bootlegging**, ran **protection rackets** and murdered rivals. They bribed the police, officials and even judges to stay out of prison. The only way to combat this crime was to end Prohibition.

## Differing attitudes towards Prohibition

REVISED

There was a lot of opposition to Prohibition:
- millions in the cities ignored it
- wealthy people supported the Association Against Prohibition Amendment (AAPA)
- the Women's Organization for National Prohibition Reform (WONPR) became the biggest anti-Prohibition organisation in the country.

While Prohibition was widely ignored in cities, it was supported in the countryside because:
- rural workers thought drunkenness was immoral
- some Protestant groups thought drinking was a sin
- middle-class communities thought alcohol made people poorer.

> **What you need to know**
>
> You need to be able to explain why Prohibition was introduced and how it led to an increase in organised crime.

> ### Revision tasks
>
> TESTED
>
> 1 Make a list of the reasons Prohibition was introduced.
> 2 Make a list of the problems Prohibition caused.
> 3 How successful do you think Prohibition was? Explain your answer.

# Reasons for the failure of Prohibition

REVISED

Why did Prohibition fail?
- Rich and powerful people opposed it.
- The government lost a lot of taxes.
- Brewing towns lost a lot of jobs.
- It increased crime.

**What you need to know**

You need to be able to explain the different reasons why Prohibition failed.

In 1929, the Wickersham Commission reported that Prohibition was unenforceable because people ignored the law. There was also anger at the rise of organised crime. In 1933, new President, Franklin D Roosevelt passed the Beer Permit Act, allowing the sale of alcohol. The 21st Amendment ended Prohibition on 5 December 1933.

Prohibition did reduce alcohol consumption by 70 per cent and alcohol-related deaths were fewer than in the 1910s.

## Exam practice

1 Why did imigrants face hostility in the USA in the 1920s? [8]

2 Describe two ways in which the law on Prohibition was broken in the USA in the 1920s. [6]

**Reasons for Prohibition**
- Temperance organisations
- Alcohol linked to poverty, violence and crime
- Need for sober workers during the First World War
- 18th Amendment begins Prohibition

**Attitudes towards Prohibition**
- Supporters of Prohibition thought it led to immorality and poverty
- Opponents of Prohibition ignored it or campaigned against it

**Reasons for the failure of Prohibition**
- Law was widely ignored
- Caused a lot of crime
- 1929: Wickersham Commission criticisms
- 1933: Beer Permit Act
- 21st Amendment ends Prohibition

**Organised crime, corruption**
- Rise of illegal, homemade 'moonshine'
- Bootlegging and racketeering
- Speakeasies and organised criminal gangs

**Summary diagram: Prohibition**

Exam practice answers at **www.hoddereducation.co.uk/myrevisionnotesdownloads**

# 3 Social change and popular entertainment

## The changing role of women in American society

REVISED

There were major changes in attitudes towards women in the 1920s.

### Voting rights for women

In 1920, Congress passed the 19th Amendment to give women the vote.

### The significance of voting rights

In 1920, the Women's Joint Congressional Committee (WJCC) **lobbied** for laws to protect women and children. The resulting 1921 Sheppard–Towner Act provided federal funding for maternity and childcare. In 1923, the Women's Bureau said the female civil servants should get equal pay to men.

### The Equal Rights Amendment, 1923

Right-wing politicians said the WJCC were communists and Christian groups said it was trying to destroy the family. The National Women's Party (NWP) proposed the Equal Rights Amendment (ERA) in 1923. This argued for completely equal rights between men and women. Congress did not pass the ERA until 1972.

### Were women more powerful?

A few women became judges in the 1920s. Nellie Tayloe Ross was elected state governor of Wyoming in 1924. But by 1930, only 13 women had been elected to Congress.

### Women in the workplace

Poor women in rural areas worked as farm labourers; in the towns they did factory work in the day but were wives and mothers at night. There were changes for other women:
- some worked in armaments (weapons) factories in the First World War
- some businesswomen achieved success, for example, Estee Lauder
- by 1930, the clerical profession (secretaries, typists, for example) was almost wholly female
- in 1920, Congress created the Women's Bureau to improve working conditions and job opportunities for women
- the Women's Trade Union League organised unions for women
- the number of women in work increased by 2 million in the 1920s.

### Significance of women's work

There were limits to how much work changed for women:
- work for poor women did not change at all
- women still did not get equal pay to men
- only 15 per cent of white and 30 per cent of black married women could get paying jobs.

---

**What you need to know**

You need to be able to explain why the lives of women began to change, but also that while there was more freedom for some women, not everyone benefited from these changes.

---

**Revision tasks**

1 Create a timeline showing events that had an impact on attitudes towards women in the 1920s.
2 Explain the significance of each of the events in the timeline that you have created.

TESTED

## The influence of the flappers

Since 1890, some women already had some freedoms but most middle-class women were more restricted. They had to wear modest clothes and could not go out without a **chaperone**.

There were a number of important changes to women's lives in the 1920s:
- women got the vote in 1920
- appliances such as vacuum cleaners and washing machines gave some women more time for themselves
- radio, records and the motor car made women aware of the world beyond the home
- films portrayed adventurous women; many women copied the looks and behaviour of movie stars.

This new self-confidence resulted in some women becoming 'flappers', who:
- were more independent
- got involved in politics
- wore looser, shorter clothes to allow greater freedom of movement; some wore men's clothes
- broke traditional rules – smoking, drinking, attending speakeasies and dancing to jazz music
- were sexually liberated; some were openly lesbian.

## Continuity in the role of women

What stopped women from having a flapper lifestyle?
- Working-class women could not afford new appliances; they had to work hard in their job and at home.
- Women who worked in factories worked too long to be able to have a wild social life.
- In the countryside, many farms had electricity, but most farmers' wives could not afford to buy new appliances.
- In the 'Bible Belt' states, people believed that God made women to be mothers and homemakers.

Most women disapproved of the flappers. The Anti-Flirt League encouraged proper behaviour in young women. However, it has been suggested that the rise in the number of divorces was a sign of growing feminism.

### Revision tasks

1 Explain the influence of the flappers on the role of women in American society.
2 Make a list of the ways that women's lives changed in the 1920s, then make another list of ways in which their lives did not change.

TESTED ☐

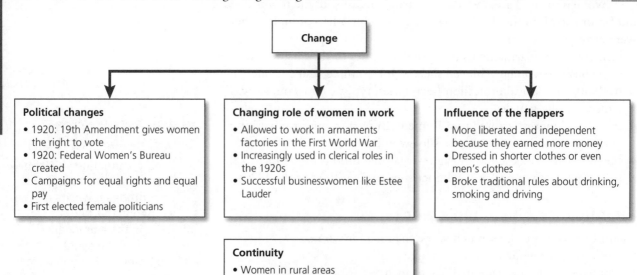

**Summary diagram:** The changing role of women in American society

# Changes in popular entertainment

Entertainment was important in the lives of Americans in the 1920s. Some of the main forms of entertainment before the 1920s were:

- **Vaudeville** – a theatre variety show featuring acts including juggling, tap dancing and singing
- dance halls – people danced the Bunny-Hug, the Turkey Trot and other new dances
- 'ragtime' – a popular form of music
- 'Nickelodeons' – cheap cinemas where people could watch early films
- baseball and college football were popular sports.

The developments in entertainment in the 1920s became known as 'the roaring twenties'.

> **What you need to know**
>
> You need to be able to explain how changes in cinema, popular music and organised sport impacted on the lives of Americans in the 1920s.

**Table 2.1 The developments in entertainment in the 1920s**

| Type of entertainment | Impact and attitudes |
|---|---|
| Jazz music – played by black musicians like Fats Waller and Duke Ellington. | • Radio and the phonograph (record-player) took jazz music into people's homes.<br>• Part of the **Harlem Renaissance**.<br>• Played in speakeasies and clubs.<br>• Popular with flappers.<br>• Some called it 'the devil's music'. |
| New dances – like the Charleston and the 'Black Bottom Stomp'. | • Associated with speakeasies.<br>• Attracted the rebellious and the young.<br>• Some thought the dances were immoral. |
| Cinema – from silent black and white films to *The Jazz Singer*, the first 'talkie', two-colour films and animations like those by Walt Disney. | • Replaced Vaudeville as the main form of popular entertainment.<br>• Taught people new fashions (such as smoking) and new ways to behave.<br>• Shocked more conservative people, leading to the Hays Code that controlled what you could show in films. |
| Radio – mass-production reduced its price; by the end of the 1920s, 10 million homes had a radio. | • Allowed people to keep up to date with news, replacing newspapers as the main source of news.<br>• Families gathered round the radio and listened to their favourite programmes together.<br>• President Roosevelt (1933–45) used the radio to give 'fireside chats' to the nation. |
| Spectator sport – baseball and boxing continued, tennis and golf were professionalised and the National Football League (NFL) was established. | • Radio made it possible for people to follow sports and teams they could never hope to go to see.<br>• Encouraged people to play sport.<br>• Made huge stars of the top players.<br>• Increased attendance at matches. |

**Jazz**
- Southern black dance music popularised by famous musicians like Fats Waller
- Radio and gramophone records helped spread this new music
- Played in the speakeasies
- Inspired new dances like the Charleston

↓

- For some jazz was the 'devil's music'
- Religious groups claimed the new dances were 'divorce feeders'

**Cinema**
- Cheap form of entertainment
- Popularity of movie stars like Charlie Chaplin
- Taught people different ways to talk and behave
- New developments like animation and sound helped keep audiences interested

↓

- Censorship was introduced to the movie industry by the Hays Code

**Spectator sport**
- The radio made it easier to follow sport and favourite teams
- The car made it easier to attend sporting events
- Sports stars like Babe Ruth helped popularise sport
- Sports were professionalised, like the NFL in 1920

↓

- Encouraged people to play sport

**Summary diagram: Changes in popular entertainment**

# 4 The 'Roaring Twenties'

## The boom years: Reasons for the rapid economic growth of the 1920s

The main causes of the economic boom of the 1920s in the USA:

### 1 The First World War

The USA was unharmed by fighting; while European factories switched to war production, US factories took over their markets; European governments borrowed billions of dollars from US banks to buy American weapons.

### 2 Mass production

American industry could produce more cheaply than other countries because the moving assembly line improved efficiency and reduced waste. American businesses bought huge quantities of materials, forcing the price down.

### 3 Mass marketing and credit

Adverts encouraged people to buy goods; travelling salesmen sold directly to people in their homes; you could buy most things by mail order.

### 4 Increasing affluence

'Hire Purchase' (buying on credit) encouraged people to borrow; average wages went up, further increasing demand.

### 5 The Stock Market

Investors bought 'shares' in companies – they got paid a '**dividend**' in return; this investment allowed US companies to expand and make even more goods.

### 6 Government policies

**Republican** Presidents believed in **laissez-faire** – giving businesses the freedom to do as they wanted; they also believed in '**rugged individualism**' – the idea that anyone could become rich simply by hard work and determination; they reduced income tax, allowed super-companies called Trusts to fix prices, weakened trade unions and workers' rights; **tariffs** like the **Fordney-McCumber Act** (1922) protected US industry from foreign competition.

### 7 The cycle of prosperity

Companies paid their workers more money as more goods were being sold. Workers went out to buy more goods because they were being paid more. Businesses and workers made each other richer. The car industry stimulated the steel, glass, tyre and oil industries.

> **What you need to know**
>
> You need to understand why the USA became so wealthy in the 1920s.

## Revision task

Put the different reasons for the economic boom into the order of how important you think they were – from the most to the least important. How would you explain your choices?

# Features of the boom and the impact on people's lives

The economic boom affected people's lives in a number of ways:

## 1 Consumer goods

There was a craze for household gadgets – for example, radios, telephones and vacuum cleaners. This helped reduce the amount of time housewives spent on housework, from 60 to 45 hours a week.

## 2 The automobile

As more people owned cars, motels, roadside 'fast-food' restaurants and drive-in movies were built; people could live on the edge of towns and drive into town centres to work and shop; motor racing became a popular sport.

## 3 The construction industry

There was a property boom in the 1920s, including skyscrapers; mansions were built for the wealthy; ordinary people bought family houses in the suburbs.

## 4 The chemicals industry

During the 1920s, the chemicals industry developed a large number of commercial products like cellophane film and Bakelite plastic.

## 5 The film industry

As more films were made, Hollywood film studios employed thousands of workers.

## 6 Mass production methods

Assembly workers found their work was repetitive and boring and they worked under great pressure.

## 7 Mass marketing and credit

Debt had become an accepted part of the American way of life. Consumer debt doubled, until it stood at $3 billion by 1930.

> **What you need to know**
>
> You need to understand how America's growing wealth in the 1920s affected people's lives.

> **Revision tasks**
>
> 1 For each impact of the economic boom listed here, write a sentence to explain how it affected people's lives.
> 2 Which impact of the economic boom do you think affected people's lives the most? Explain your choice.
>
> TESTED

---

**Reasons for the rapid economic growth in the 1920s**

- The First World War boosted US industry and removed foreign competition
- Mass production made goods cheaper
- Advertising and access to cheap credit allowed people to 'buy now, pay later'
- The cycle of prosperity – as businesses sold more they paid their workers more so they could buy more

**Policies of the Republican presidents**

- Tariffs like the Fordney-McCumber Act in 1922 helped to protect American business from foreign competition
- Laissez-faire attitudes meant that the government did not interfere in business
- Presidents reduced taxes and weakened union and worker rights to help businesses

**Impact of the boom on people's lives**

- New production techniques and materials like Bakelite created new consumer items
- Household gadgets freed housewives from housework
- Cars allowed people to live in the suburbs and commute; led to building of motels and fast-food restaurants
- Credit allowed people to buy more goods but also increased debt

**Summary diagram:** The 'Roaring Twenties'

# 5 Economic problems in the 1920s

## Problems behind the prosperity

There were a number of serious economic problems in America in the 1920s.

### 1 Decline in the 'old industries'

The growth of new industries in the 1920s left older industries facing problems.

### 2 Coal

Oil began to replace coal as a source of power and demand from the railroads also fell. The result was overproduction of coal and its price fell. Jobs in mining were also hit by increased **mechanisation**.

### 3 Textiles

Cotton mills found themselves facing competition from new materials like rayon, and falling demand because new fashions used less cloth. Instead of modernising, firms simply closed down.

### 4 Problems in agriculture

In the 1920s, the government encouraged farmers to modernise their methods, to introduce machines and better breeds and seeds. The result was overproduction, which lowered prices and profits. Prohibition destroyed the market for wheat and barley. High tariffs forced other countries to impose high tariffs on American wheat. Farming was also hit by disease like the **boll-weevil** that attacked cotton crops. Farms were sold and workers left the countryside to work in towns.

### 5 The unequal distribution of wealth

There were many people who did not prosper in the 1920s.
- Mechanisation resulted in many people losing their jobs; these people and their families lived in poverty.
- Falling wages in farming, coal and textiles left many living in poverty.
- Most black Americans suffered discrimination in low-paying, menial jobs.
- Native Americans lived in poverty on the reservations.

By 1929, 60 per cent of Americans lived in poverty. By the end of the decade, the top 5 per cent of the population owned one-third of the wealth. This was very damaging as the rich saved their money rather than spend it and the poor had no money to spend.

### 6 Overproduction and underconsumption

The main problems in the US economy by the end of the 1920s were overproduction (which flooded the market and reduced prices and therefore profits) and underconsumption (which reduced sales and therefore profits). The boom began to slow down.

> **What you need to know**
>
> You need to be able to explain why there were serious problems with the American economy in the 1920s.

American businesses could still have grown if they could sell their goods to other countries. However, other countries had raised tariffs on American goods just as America had raised tariffs on foreign goods. This meant there were too many goods for sale in America which reduced prices. The profits of US industries began to fall.

## Revision tasks

TESTED

1 Create a spider diagram showing the economic problems in America in the 1920s.
2 Explain the impact of the unequal distribution of wealth on the American economy in the 1920s.

## Exam practice

3 Below are two methods that helped to create the boom in the American economy in the 1920s.

Choose one method and explain how it helped the American economy to grow in the 1920s. [6]

| Mass production | Mass marketing and credit |
|---|---|

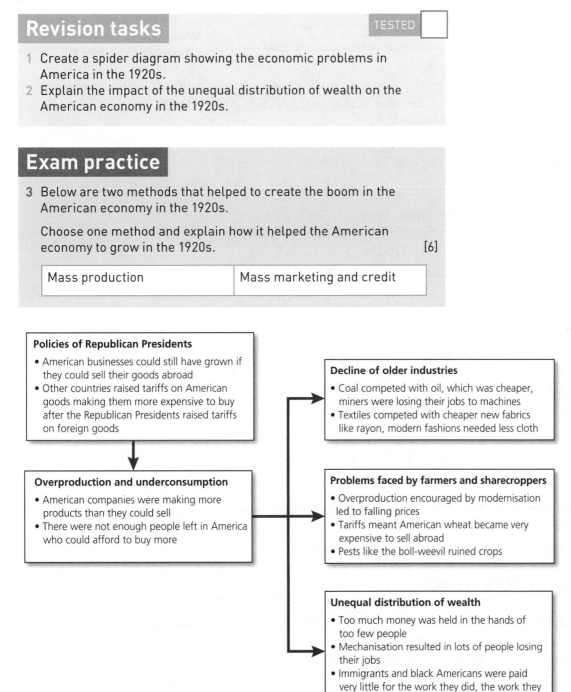

**Policies of Republican Presidents**
- American businesses could still have grown if they could sell their goods abroad
- Other countries raised tariffs on American goods making them more expensive to buy after the Republican Presidents raised tariffs on foreign goods

**Overproduction and underconsumption**
- American companies were making more products than they could sell
- There were not enough people left in America who could afford to buy more

**Decline of older industries**
- Coal competed with oil, which was cheaper, miners were losing their jobs to machines
- Textiles competed with cheaper new fabrics like rayon, modern fashions needed less cloth

**Problems faced by farmers and sharecroppers**
- Overproduction encouraged by modernisation led to falling prices
- Tariffs meant American wheat became very expensive to sell abroad
- Pests like the boll-weevil ruined crops

**Unequal distribution of wealth**
- Too much money was held in the hands of too few people
- Mechanisation resulted in lots of people losing their jobs
- Immigrants and black Americans were paid very little for the work they did, the work they were offered was limited

**Summary diagram:** Economic problems in the 1920s

# 6 The Wall Street Crash, 1929

## The Wall Street Crash of October 1929

REVISED

Investors buy 'shares' in a company. The company uses this money to increase the value of its business by researching new products or buying new machinery.

Shareholders get paid a dividend, a share of this increased value. Shareholders sell their shares in a company when the price is higher. The more a company is worth, the higher the value of its shares. **Speculators** make a living just from buying and selling shares.

Between 1924 and 1929 the price of shares on the New York **Stock Exchange** on Wall Street rose by 500 per cent.

### Causes of the Crash

People thought prices would keep on rising forever. Many borrowed money to buy shares, hoping to pay back the loan with the profit they made when they sold their shares ('**buying on the margin**'). As a result, share prices rose faster than the value of the companies. Banks were happy to lend their customers' savings to speculators as they were sure they would make their money back.

### Events of the Crash

In early September 1929, there were repeated warnings of a crash and prices began to fall. The more prices fell, the more people wanted to sell and so prices fell faster.

Thursday 24 October ('Black Thursday'): 13 million shares sold; because there were few buyers, prices crashed.

Friday 25 October: Bankers bought shares to restore confidence.

Monday 28 October: 9 million shares were sold; prices continued to fall.

Tuesday 29 October: 6 million shares were sold in a panic for anything they could get.

November: Share prices continued to fall until mid-November.

## The effects of the Crash

REVISED

Shareholders lost $8 billion in one day on 29 October. Most people did not own any shares. However, the Crash affected the economy which had a knock-on effect on most Americans during the 1930s.

Spreading effects:
- The banks – much of the speculation had been financed by the banks. When speculators failed to pay back their loans, many banks went bankrupt. By 1933, 5,000 American banks had failed and their customers had lost all of their money.
- The economy – people stopped spending. Sales of essentials did not fall by much, but sales of cars and labour-saving devices which people could live without plummeted.
- The world – American banks began calling in foreign loans, which caused a financial crises in Europe. Europeans stopped buying goods from abroad. This damaged American exports and made the position of American companies even worse.

---

**What you need to know**

You need to be able to explain what the Wall Street Crash was and why it happened.

---

**Revision tasks**

1. How would you describe the Wall Street Crash to someone who did not know what it was?
2. List the main causes of the Wall Street Crash.

TESTED

---

**What you need to know**

You need to explain how the Crash affected US banks and businesses and how this led to an economic depression that lasted through the 1930s.

---

# The cycle of depression

Companies closed down factories and laid off workers. This led to the 'cycle of depression' (see below). Falling demand led to increased unemployment, which reduced demand further.

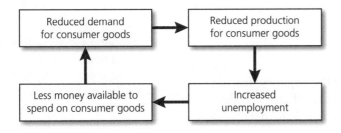

# The government made things worse

The government's lack of economic understanding made problems worse.

1 The **US Federal Reserve** raised interest rates which stopped borrowing.
2 The government kept to the '**Gold Standard**', which limited the money that people had to spend.
3 The 1930 Hawley–Smoot Act increased tariffs which decreased international trade even further.

# The end of confidence

The confidence of the boom had gone. People were more careful about how they spent their money. This held back the economic growth that would have solved the situation as spending money would have meant businesses could have stayed open and people could have kept their jobs.

## Revision tasks
TESTED

1 What do you think was the most serious effect of the Wall Street Crash? Explain your choice.
2 List the main effects of the Wall Street Crash.
3 How successful was the US Government in dealing with the Wall Street Crash in 1929?

**Causes**
• People borrowed money to buy shares
• The value of shares rose faster than companies could increase their profits
• When share prices started to fall people started to sell their shares, pushing prices down further

| Date | Events |
|---|---|
| 24 October 1929 | 'Black Thursday' 13 million shares sold; prices crashed |
| 25 October 1929 | Bankers bought shares to restore confidence |
| 28 October 1929 | nine million shares sold |
| 29 October 1929 | six million shares sold |
| November 1929 | Share prices fell until mid-November |

**Effects**
• Many banks went bankrupt
• People stopped spending on anything except essentials
• Banks called in foreign loans causing other countries to have financial difficulties
• The cycle of depression – businesses failed, workers became unemployed, less money was spent, more businesses closed

**Summary diagram: The Wall Street Crash, 1929**

# 7 The Great Depression, 1929–33

## The Great Depression and its effects on industry and workers

REVISED

### Closures and unemployment

By the end of 1932, 10,000 banks had failed. There were 'runs on the banks', where everybody tried to withdraw their money, fearing that the banks were about to go bankrupt. The four-day 'Bank Holiday' in 1933 allowed the government to check that banks were financially stable.

One hundred thousand businesses shut down between 1929 and 1932. The number of unemployed rose to almost 13 million (a quarter of the working population) in 1933. It was particularly bad for women, unskilled and black workers. The 'old industries' were particularly badly hit. Textile, car, iron and steel production all fell.

### The 'new industries'

Prices halved, so people who had a job could buy more with their money. The 'new industries' (such as electrical goods, chemicals) continued to expand. They invested so they could cut costs and reduce prices.

### Poverty and hunger

America had a very limited welfare system, which the poverty of the Depression overwhelmed. Soup kitchens, 'breadlines' of people waiting for food and men begging for a job, became common features of American towns. Between 1931 and 1933, there were hunger marches all over the USA. The marchers were met with force, for example in 1932, a peaceful march of 5,000 people in Detroit was attacked by police and guards from the Ford Automobile Company.

### Hoovervilles

Hoovervilles were shanty towns, built of packing boxes and corrugated iron sheets, named after President Hoover.

People who lived there looked after each other when they could not look after themselves. Some lived in tiny shacks, others had to sleep rough.

### The Bonus Army

In 1924, Congress had voted to give each First World War veteran a bonus which was to have been paid by 1944. In January 1932, a 'Bonus Army' of 25,000 men marched on Washington to claim their bonus. They set up a Hooverville, military-style, with strict hygiene rules and a daily parade. In July, President Hoover sent in 600 troops and tanks to break up the camp. Congress finally paid the bonus in 1936.

---

**What you need to know**

You need to be able to explain how the Depression affected the lives of businesses and workers in American towns and cities in the 1930s.

---

**Revision tasks**

1 Make a list of all the problems that the Depression caused for businesses and workers.
2 Did anyone benefit from the Depression?
3 Why do you think President Hoover's treatment of the Bonus Army was unpopular with the American people?

TESTED

# The Great Depression and its effects on agriculture and the lives of farmers

REVISED

## Effects of tariffs and overproduction

Agriculture struggled during the 1920s as overproduction drove down the price of food. The hard times of 1929–33 caused a collapse in demand for food. American tariffs on foreign imports meant that other countries put tariffs on American farming produce. Farmers found it more difficult to sell their produce abroad.

Many had taken out large loans to mechanise their farms. Farmers who had bought shares were ruined by the Crash. Many rural banks failed.

## Hardships of farmers and sharecroppers

Many farmers went bankrupt – farms were **foreclosed** or sold off.

Large industrial-scale farms replaced smaller farms. Farmer-owners became paid labourers.

Sharecroppers were badly hit in the southern states, where white workers pressured landowners to give them work instead. Landowners reduced their rates to force black sharecroppers off the land.

## Farming problems in the Midwest

In the 1930s the Midwest saw record summer temperatures and the worst drought in 300 years. In 1935 it rained at harvest time, ruining the crop. Pests thrived; there was a plague of chinch bugs in 1933 and grasshoppers in 1936.

During the 1920s, farmers in the Midwest had overcropped the fields, trying to get more money by growing more. This had drained the soil of nutrients. Crops failed in the drought which created huge dust storms which blew for hundreds of miles, destroying people's homes and farms. This forced many people to leave these areas.

## Okies and hobos

Many farmers and labourers were driven off the land. The 'Okies' came from Oklahoma to work on the fruit farms of California. They lived in filthy shanty towns. Many of them died from disease. Others became hobos, seeking work from farm to farm either by walking or jumping onto slow-moving trains.

## The farmers fight back

Some farmers tried to resist the developments.
- The 1932 Iowa Farm War – farmers tried to force up prices by agreeing to sell nothing.
- The 1931 Nebraska 'Penny Auctions' – people turned up at foreclosure auctions for farms and deliberately put in low bids.
- The 1932 Alabama Croppers and Farm Workers Union (CFWU) – demanded a better rate for cotton.

States tried to persuade farmers to 'Live at Home'. The Governor of North Carolina tried to reduce the amount of land given over to tobacco and cotton by encouraging farmers to grow their own food.

Option 2 Life in the United States of America, 1920–33

---

**What you need to know**

You need to be able to explain how the Depression affected the lives of farmers in the American countryside in the 1930s.

---

## Revision tasks

1 Explain how the following factors caused problems for American farmers in the 1930s:
- tariffs
- overproduction
- mechanisation
- the weather
- pests
- overcropping.
2 Which problem do you think was most serious for American farmers? Explain your choice

TESTED

# Republican beliefs and policies

REVISED

Republican Presidents in the 1920s like Herbert Hoover (1929–33) believed in:

- laissez-faire – not interfering in the economy
- 'rugged individualism' – people should sort out their own problems
- 'voluntarism' – charities should help the poor, not the government.

These ideas seemed to work well during the boom, but left many people poor and starving during the Depression.

**What you need to know**

You need to be able to explain how Republicans like President Hoover tried to respond to the Depression and how effective his actions were.

# The impact and effectiveness of Hoover's policies and actions

REVISED

## President Hoover and the Great Depression

People thought President Hoover did not do anything to help solve the problems of the Depression. This is not true; however, what he did try to do often did not work.

- The Federal Farm Board was set up in 1929 to buy surplus farm produce to keep prices up, but encouraged farmers to grow too much.
- Hoover restricted the money supply by sticking to the gold standard.
- He increased interest rates which made borrowing more expensive.
- The 1930 Hawley-Smoot Act set a tariff on imported products. When other countries did the same to American products it damaged US businesses which depended on selling abroad.
- The 1931 President's Organization on Unemployment Relief (POUR), advised charities how to help the unemployed and encouraged fund-raising. Charity donations almost doubled in 1931 but they were overwhelmed with demand for their services.
- In 1932, the government offered loans to the states to provide unemployment pay, but states did not want to increase their debt.
- The 1932 Norris-La Guardia Act allowed workers to join unions and to strike, but workers did not feel secure enough to try and pressure their bosses.

Some of Hoover's policies, like the 1932 Reconstruction Finance Corporation (RFC) which offered loans to banks and companies that were struggling, and spending on road-building, public buildings and the Hoover Dam, were similar to those in Roosevelt's New Deal (see page 47) but did not do enough to stop the Depression.

## Hoover's unpopularity

As the Depression continued, Hoover became increasingly unpopular.

Hoover believed in a 'balanced budget', so he had to increase taxes to pay for his public works. His 1932 Revenue Act introduced an income tax – the rate increased depending on how much money you earned; this made him unpopular with rich people who now had to pay 63 per cent tax instead of the 25 per cent they paid before. His proposed Sales Tax made him more unpopular with the poor.

The Democratic Party blamed Hoover for the Depression, with slogans like 'In Hoover we trusted, now we are busted'. They invented a series of 'Hoover' terms that attacked his reputation. For example:

- the 'Hoover blanket' – a newspaper used as a blanket
- 'Hoover leather' – cardboard used to fill a hole in a shoe
- 'Hoover stew' – soup from a soup kitchen.

As well as this, the attack on the Bonus Army in 1932 was seen as an attack on war heroes.

**Revision tasks**

1 List the key actions that President Hoover took to attempt to solve the problems of the Great Depression.

2 How successful were President Hoover's policies in solving the problems of the Great Depression? Why was this?

TESTED

## The 1932 Presidential election

Hoover was very unpopular. During the election campaign, people booed films of him in the cinema, his train had eggs thrown at it and the Secret Service had to stop a number of assassination attempts.

Franklin D Roosevelt, Hoover's Democrat opponent, was very popular. Roosevelt blamed the bankers and the rich, which appealed to poor people. He promised 'a New Deal for the American people'. This meant:
● public works programmes
● welfare
● support for industry and agriculture
● banking reform.

He offered people hope.

In the 1932 election, Roosevelt won by 23 million votes (42 States) to Hoover's 16 million votes (six States).

## Exam practice

4 Below is a list of words linked with the Wall Street Crash in October 1929:

| Black Tuesday | J P Morgan | Black Thursday | Herbert Hoover | On the margin |
|---|---|---|---|---|

Match each word to the correct description.
a System of paying only 10% of the price of a share and borrowing the rest [1]
b Banker who tried to restore confidence [1]
c President at the time of the Wall Street Crash [1]
d Day when most shares were sold before the crash on Wall Street [1]
e Day of the Wall Street Crash [1]

5 'The Great Depression had more impact on the lives of farmers than on the lives of workers in the period 1929–33'.
Do you agree? Explain your answer. [16]

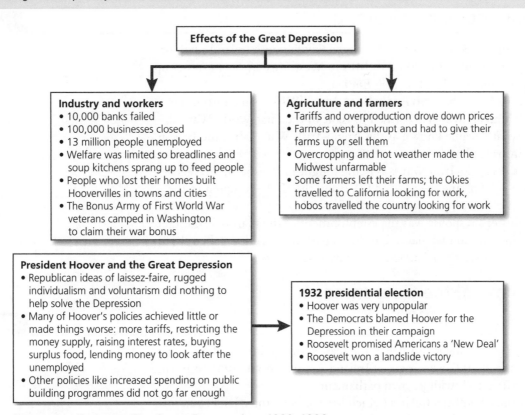

**Industry and workers**
● 10,000 banks failed
● 100,000 businesses closed
● 13 million people unemployed
● Welfare was limited so breadlines and soup kitchens sprang up to feed people
● People who lost their homes built Hoovervilles in towns and cities
● The Bonus Army of First World War veterans camped in Washington to claim their war bonus

**Agriculture and farmers**
● Tariffs and overproduction drove down prices
● Farmers went bankrupt and had to give their farms up or sell them
● Overcropping and hot weather made the Midwest unfarmable
● Some farmers left their farms; the Okies travelled to California looking for work, hobos travelled the country looking for work

**President Hoover and the Great Depression**
● Republican ideas of laissez-faire, rugged individualism and voluntarism did nothing to help solve the Depression
● Many of Hoover's policies achieved little or made things worse: more tariffs, restricting the money supply, raising interest rates, buying surplus food, lending money to look after the unemployed
● Other policies like increased spending on public building programmes did not go far enough

**1932 presidential election**
● Hoover was very unpopular
● The Democrats blamed Hoover for the Depression in their campaign
● Roosevelt promised Americans a 'New Deal'
● Roosevelt won a landslide victory

**Summary diagram:** The Great Depression, 1929–1933

## 1 The partitioning of Ireland

### Ireland before partition

REVISED

Ireland was ruled from **Westminster** between 1801 and 1920. For much of this time:

- **nationalist** politicians in Ireland demanded **home rule** by a parliament in Dublin
- the **unionist** population (mainly in the north-eastern part of the island) opposed home rule.

In 1912, Britain's government agreed to introduce home rule to Ireland by 1914. This led both the nationalists and the unionists to set up private armies:

- the nationalists set up the Irish Volunteers
- the unionists established the **Ulster Volunteer Force (UVF)**.

However, because of the start of the First World War in August 1914, the introduction of home rule was agreed to be postponed until after the war. Although both sides agreed to send their private armies to fight for the Allies in the war, some of the Irish Volunteers refused to go.

In April 1916, a nationalist rebellion (the Easter Rising) was staged and Ireland was declared a republic. Though the rebellion failed, the harsh reaction of the British increased the nationalist demand for full independence.

> **What you need to know**
>
> While this information will not be examined, it is important that you know the background to the establishment of Northern Ireland and the key terms of the Government of Ireland Act.

### The partitioning of Ireland

REVISED

Following the 1918 **general election**, *Sinn Féin* became Ireland's largest political party. Rather than send its MPs to Westminster, *Sinn Féin* set up its own parliament in Dublin, *Dáil Éireann*.

- In January 1919, the **Irish Republican Army (IRA)**, formed from the Irish Volunteers who had refused to fight in the First World War, began what became known as the Anglo-Irish War against the British forces in Ireland.
- While the Anglo-Irish War was being fought in the south, **sectarian** violence – involving the revived UVF and the IRA – erupted in the northern counties, particularly in Belfast and Derry/Londonderry.
- Westminster's response was the establishment of the mainly Protestant Ulster Special Constabulary. This had a part-time section called the B Specials who were particularly feared by nationalists.

### Key terms of the Government of Ireland Act, 1920

REVISED

The British government also began the search for a political solution. The result was the 1920 Government of Ireland Act which **partitioned** Ireland into two parts, each with its own parliament:

- a 26-county Southern Ireland (which later became the **Irish Free State**)
- a six-county Northern Ireland.

These parliaments were given control over areas such as education, health and transport. Westminster would keep responsibility for defence, foreign policy and taxation. The use of **Proportional Representation** (PR) would protect minorities.

Both areas would still send some MPs to Westminster while the monarch would be represented by a single **Viceroy**. Later, when the 1921 Treaty was signed, the position of Viceroy was replaced by that of Governor of Northern Ireland.

The Act also established a Council of Ireland made up of 20 politicians from each parliament. It would have the power over issues such as fishing and trade. If both parliaments agreed, these powers could be increased, thus helping to bring about reunification.

## Reactions to the Government of Ireland Act in the north and south of Ireland

The Government of Ireland Act delighted unionists, as it gave them control over their own affairs. They quickly organised elections for their new parliament and their leader, Sir James Craig, became Prime Minister.

The creation of Northern Ireland was bitterly opposed by most nationalists living there:
- many were convinced that partition would not last and so they refused to recognise the new state
- as a result, unionists believed that nationalists wanted to destroy Northern Ireland.

The high levels of sectarian violence in the early months of Northern Ireland's existence increased each side's doubts and suspicions.

The terms of the Act were unacceptable to Irish Republicans:
- they used the terms of the Act to elect a second *Dáil* and the Anglo-Irish War continued
- in July 1921, both sides agreed a ceasefire and in December 1921 they signed the Anglo-Irish Treaty. This established the Irish Free State as a **dominion** of the **British Commonwealth**.

Although it was still not full independence, the Anglo-Irish Treaty gave Dublin more power than the Government of Ireland Act had done. However, the Treaty divided Irish Republicans. There were two problems:

**Table 3.1 Problems with the Anglo-Irish Treaty**

| Continuation of strong links with the British Commonwealth | Confirmation of the partitioning of Ireland as introduced by the 1920 Government of Ireland Act |
| --- | --- |
| By signing the Treaty, the Irish accepted continued links with the UK with:<br>- an oath of allegiance to the British monarch, sworn by members of the Irish Parliament.<br>- the appointment of a **Governor General** to represent the monarch in the Irish Free State.<br>- the right of Irish Free State citizens to appeal judgements of Irish courts to the British **Privy Council**.<br><br>In addition, Britain kept three military bases in Berehaven, Cobh (both in County Cork) and Lough Swilly (County Donegal). | *Sinn Féin* had reluctantly accepted partition due to the British Prime Minister's promise to set up a Boundary Commission to examine the location of the border at a future date.<br><br>They believed that this commission would take land from Northern Ireland and leave it too small to survive. This promise did not convince all Republicans.<br><br>The anti-treaty members of *Sinn Féin* attacked the Treaty for accepting partition. They argued that it meant the abandonment of half a million nationalists living inside Northern Ireland. |

Revision tasks

1 Create a timeline showing the key events in Ireland 1912–20.
2 Create a spider diagram showing the main terms of the 1920 Government of Ireland Act.

TESTED ☐

REVISED ☐

**What you need to know**

There were very different reactions to the Government of Ireland Act between nationalists and unionists – and to the Anglo-Irish Treaty within nationalism. Make sure you can explain why there were such different views.

Option 1 Changing Relations: Northern Ireland and its Neighbours, 1920–49

# The setting up of the Irish Free State

REVISED

Republican divisions were so serious that a **civil war** was fought from 1922 to 1923. The pro-treaty side won and, under the leadership of *Cumann na nGaedheal*, the Free State set about establishing the new state and increasing its independence from Britain.

This ended with the 1931 Statute of Westminster, which stated that dominions were independent countries that could leave the Commonwealth without Britain's permission. In 1926, de Valera left *Sinn Féin* and established *Fianna Fáil*. *Fianna Fáil* entered the *Dáil* in 1927 and became the **official opposition** party.

**What you need to know**

The Irish Free State experienced a lot of upheaval in its first decade. Make sure that you have a clear understanding of the key events of these years and why the **Statute of Westminster** was so important.

## The Boundary Commission, 1924–25

The Boundary Commission finally met in 1925. It did not change the border; indeed, it actually recommended giving some Irish Free State land to Northern Ireland.

All sides therefore agreed to shelve the Commission report in favour of an Anglo-Irish Agreement, whereby:
- the border would remain unchanged and the powers of the Council of Ireland would pass to the Belfast parliament
- the Free State was let off making contributions to the UK's national debt as agreed to in the 1921 Treaty
- Northern Ireland was relieved from paying any more **land annuities**.

From that point it became clear that partition was permanent and so nationalist MPs started to attend the Northern Ireland Parliament.

## Revision tasks

TESTED

1 Create a table explaining the Government of Ireland Act using the following headings:
   - Unionist reaction
   - Northern nationalist reaction
   - Irish republican reaction
2 Create a spider diagram showing the key elements of the 1921 Anglo-Irish Treaty.
3 Create a timeline showing the key events in Ireland 1921–31.

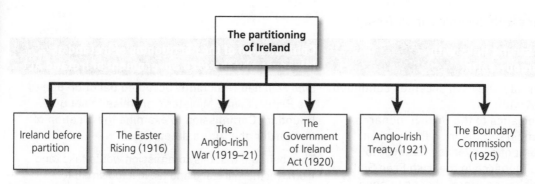

**Summary diagram:** The partitioning of Ireland

# 2 From Irish Free State to Éire

## De Valera and his role in the dismantling of the Anglo-Irish Treaty by 1937

REVISED

Following a general election in March 1932, *Fianna Fáil* took power. De Valera soon moved to change things.

- The IRA was legalised and began to organise openly again, even attacking *Cumann na nGaedheal* members, who responded by setting up the Army Comrades Association (ACA – also known as the Blueshirts). In 1933, *Cumann na nGaedheal* and the Blueshirts joined together to form a new party, *Fine Gael*. In 1936, de Valera responded to IRA activities by declaring the organisation illegal.
- In November 1932, London recalled its Governor General, James MacNeill as *Fianna Fáil* ministers were snubbing him. His replacement was a *Fianna Fáil* politician, Domhnall O'Buachalla. He did not use the title of Governor General, and he undertook no official duties – except signing bills passed by the *Dáil* into law.
- The Removal of the Oath Act (passed in May 1933) eliminated the Oath of Allegiance to the British Monarch.
- In May 1933, the Constitution was changed to stop people appealing Irish Court verdicts to the Privy Council. In 1935, London challenged these actions before the Privy Council. It ruled that the 1931 Statute of Westminster gave de Valera the power to make such changes.
- De Valera used the 1936 **abdication crisis** to pass:
  - the Constitution Act – which removed all reference to the British monarch and the Governor General from the constitution
  - the External Relations Act – which ended the monarch's official role within the Free State.

> **What you need to know**
>
> After coming to power in 1932, de Valera made it his mission to remove all possible links with the Commonwealth. It is important that you can explain what he did and how London reacted.

> **What you need to know**
>
> Changing a country's Constitution is a really big deal. You must be able to explain the changes that were made and what impact they had – particularly on relations with the United Kingdom and Northern Ireland.

## The reasons for and terms of the 1937 Constitution

REVISED

All these changes made the Irish Free State's Constitution out of date. In 1937, therefore, de Valera introduced a new constitution, *Bunreacht na hÉireann* which included three significant changes:

1. The Irish Free State would henceforth be known as Éire.
2. The title of the head of government would be **Taoiseach**.
3. The (mainly ceremonial) head of state would be the President. The position would be decided by an election, held every seven years.

The key terms of the 1937 constitution were as follows:

1. Irish was recognised as the official language.
2. The Catholic Church was given a 'special position', although 'freedom of conscience and the free profession and practice of religion' was granted to other faiths.
3. Article II claimed the right to rule over the whole island.
4. Article III added that until partition ended, Éire's laws would only apply to the 26 counties currently governed by Dublin.

Nowhere in the new constitution was the British monarch mentioned. Éire had become a republic in all but name, yet the country still remained part of the Commonwealth because de Valera believed that breaking the link would make partition even harder to end.

> **Revision tasks**
>
> 1 Create a table showing the key actions taken by de Valera 1932–1936 using the headings:
> - Action
> - Reason
> - Impact
> 2 Create a spider diagram showing the main terms of the 1937 Constitution.
>
>
> TESTED

# The impact of the 1937 Constitution on relations between Britain, Northern Ireland and Éire

REVISED

While London decided that these changes did not alter its relationship with Dublin, *Bunreacht na hÉireann* reinforced unionists' determination to remain within the UK. The unionist government – based at **Stormont** since 1932 – strongly criticised *Bunreacht na hÉireann*. In particular it:

1 condemned Article II
2 denounced the particular mention of the position of the Catholic Church and the Irish language.

Lord Craigavon used the opportunity to call a snap general election in 1938, resulting in an increased majority for his party.

Some historians believe that northern nationalists also had a lot to be dissatisfied with. Despite the inclusion of Articles II and III, it could be argued that, by removing almost all links with Britain and the Commonwealth, the new constitution had actually strengthened partition.

## Revision task

How did the following groups react to *Bunreacht na hÉireann*?
- British government
- Unionists
- Northern nationalists

TESTED

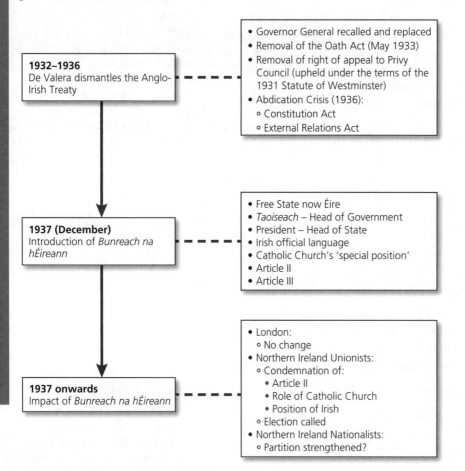

**1932–1936**
De Valera dismantles the Anglo-Irish Treaty

- Governor General recalled and replaced
- Removal of the Oath Act (May 1933)
- Removal of right of appeal to Privy Council (upheld under the terms of the 1931 Statute of Westminster)
- Abdication Crisis (1936):
  - Constitution Act
  - External Relations Act

**1937 (December)**
Introduction of *Bunreach na hÉireann*

- Free State now Éire
- *Taoiseach* – Head of Government
- President – Head of State
- Irish official language
- Catholic Church's 'special position'
- Article II
- Article III

**1937 onwards**
Impact of *Bunreach na hÉireann*

- London:
  - No change
- Northern Ireland Unionists:
  - Condemnation of:
    - Article II
    - Role of Catholic Church
    - Position of Irish
  - Election called
- Northern Ireland Nationalists:
  - Partition strengthened?

**Summary diagrm:** From Irish Free State to Éire

# 3 The Economic War

Land reform had been one of the biggest issues in nineteenth-century Irish history. The 1870 Land Act tried to solve the problem by lending tenants money to buy land they worked. Each year the farmers paid back part of the loan (known as land annuities).

## The causes of the Economic War

REVISED

Between 1922 and 1932 this money was collected by the Irish government and sent on to London. Irish farmers disliked paying annuities and following his election, de Valera stopped these payments. He argued that:

- the Irish economy was suffering from the economic depression
- London had stopped Northern Ireland's land annuities. Free State farmers should be treated the same.

Britain responded by imposing **duties** of 20 per cent on Free State imports. The Irish government then:

- called a snap general election in January 1933. This gave de Valera more seats, thus strengthening his position
- imposed similar duties on imports from Great Britain and Northern Ireland.

The standoff (known as the Economic War) continued for six years, although in 1935 both sides agreed a Coal–Cattle Pact that made trade in these two commodities much easier.

> ### What you need to know
>
> The Economic War was a major element of Anglo-Irish relations in the 1930s. It is important that you can explain why it started, what impact it had and how and why it ended.

## The effects of the Economic War

REVISED

As 90 per cent of Irish exports went to Britain, this war had a significant impact.

- While the government benefited from keeping the annuities, Irish farmers probably suffered most with a 35 per cent reduction in cattle exports (from 1929 levels), due to less trade with both Great Britain and Northern Ireland, resulting in massive overproduction of beef.
- Alternative export markets were not available due to the ongoing World Depression; as a consequence, many farmers went bankrupt.
- The Irish government offered **subsidies** to encourage farmers to increase production of new crops such as sugar beet and wheat. This met with limited success as such crops were grown at the expense of others, such as barley, and it was only the bigger farmers who made the switch. As a result, living standards fell even though taxes were raised to compensate farmers. At the same time, smaller-scale farmers did benefit from the reduction in the annuity payments, now made to the Dublin government.

De Valera hoped that taxing British goods would encourage the development of Irish industries. This did not really happen due to a lack of investment. Any new companies set up were not really geared towards exports and as a result the economy experienced a **trade deficit** and there were cutbacks in electricity generation and rail transport. On the other hand, the lack of UK coal did result in a period of growth for Ireland's peat industry. Additionally, new cement factories were established, while the government spent £1 million on improving bridges and rural cottages.

> ### Revision task
>
> Explain the Economic War using these headings:
> - Land annuities pre–1922
> - Land annuities 1922–32
> - Why de Valera stopped payments
> - British response
> - Irish response
>
> TESTED

## The impact on relations between Northern Ireland and Britain

The Economic War led to a deterioration in Anglo-Irish relations.
● Economically it had a much greater impact on Northern Ireland than on Britain, although there is some evidence that unemployment in Britain did increase.
● While Britain had many other markets for its goods, much of Northern Ireland's economic prosperity depended on strong cross-border trade with the Free State and this was hit by de Valera's import duties. All such trade stopped during the Economic War, although smuggling increased.

Northern Ireland's farmers, however, were helped by being able to provide Britain with produce no longer supplied by the Irish Free State.

## The end of the Economic War

British Prime Minister Neville Chamberlain decided that Anglo-Irish relations needed to improve. This would mean:
● ending the Economic War
● resolving the issue of the treaty ports.

Chamberlain recognised the ports' strategic value, but he also knew that they were out of date. He therefore decided that returning them would help end the Economic War and result in Éire's assistance if war broke out. Keen to get the ports back, de Valera believed that Britain's continued control would weaken Éire's claims to neutrality and leave her open to attack.

## The terms of the Anglo-Irish Agreements of 1938 and their significance for relations between Britain, Northern Ireland and Éire

REVISED ☐

Representatives of the two governments began to talk in January 1938. On 25 April 1938, the two governments signed agreements on defence, finance and trade. As a result, the Economic War was ended:
● the treaty ports were returned to Éire
● Éire agreed to pay Britain £10 million to resolve the annuities question
● all duties imposed by both countries during the Economic War were removed.

The end to the trade war did not apply to cross-border trade with Northern Ireland, however a three-year trade agreement between Éire and Northern Ireland was also reached. Overall, de Valera was delighted with the outcome of the agreements.

Winston Churchill was critical of the return of the treaty ports as he did not share Chamberlain's belief that Éire would allow Britain to use the ports during a future war.

## Revision task

Examine the impact of the Economic War by writing a sentence on each of the following:
● impact on the Irish economy
● impact on the British economy
● impact on the Northern Irish economy
● impact on relations between Britain, Northern Ireland and Ireland.

TESTED ☐

REVISED ☐

### What you need to know

Examiners will expect you to be able to explain the terms of the 1938 Anglo-Irish Agreements and what these terms meant for relations between Britain, Northern Ireland and Éire.

Unionists were also unhappy.

● Craigavon agreed with Churchill's view that the return of the treaty ports would weaken the security of both the UK and Éire.
● He feared the improvement in Anglo-Irish relations might lead to the reunification of Ireland.

Chamberlain attempted to calm Craigavon by making concessions on agricultural subsidies and with the promise of an increased share of weapons manufacture.

## Exam practice

1 Study Source A below and answer the question which follows:

### Source A

> To me this treaty gives me what I and my colleagues fought for; it gives us for the first time in 700 years, the evacuation of Britain's armed forces out of Ireland.
>
> Seán MacEoin gives a supporter's view of the Treaty, December 1921.

Using Source A and your contextual knowledge, give one reason which explains why some Republicans supported the 1921 Treaty. [2]

---

**Causes of the Economic War**
● Dislike of land annuities:
  ○ 1922–32 – collected by Dublin government and sent to London
● De Valera stops paying land annuities:
  ○ Impact of Economic Depression
  ○ Northern Ireland not paying annuities
● London's response:
  ○ Imposition of duties
● De Valera's response:
  ○ Snap election
  ○ Imposition of duties

**Effects of the Economic War**
● Dublin government benefited from keeping annuities
● Impact on Irish farmers:
  ○ 35% reduction in cattle exports – overproduction of beef
  ○ Lack of alternative markets – Depression
  ○ Limited impact of subsidies to grow new crops
  ○ Fall in living standards
● Impact on Irish industry:
  ○ Failure to develop industries due to lack of investment except peat/cement
● Trade deficit
● Impact on relations with Northern Ireland and Britain:
  ○ Deterioration in relations:
    ▪ Limited impact on Britain
    ▪ Significant impact on Northern Ireland

**End of the Economic War**
● Reasons for ending the war:
  ● Chamberlain
  ● De Valera
● Terms of the Anglo-Irish Agreements:
  ○ Defence
  ○ Finance
  ○ Trade
● Significance of Anglo-Irish Agreements:
  ● Opposition from:
    ● Churchill
    ● Northern Ireland Unionists

**Summary diagram:** The Economic War

# 4 Northern Ireland and World War II

On 1 September 1939, Germany invaded Poland. The Second World War began two days later.

## Northern Ireland's reaction to the outbreak of war

REVISED

The Stormont government stated its readiness to play its part in the forthcoming war effort, hoping to strengthen its union with Great Britain.

## Differing attitudes towards conscription

REVISED

In April 1939, London announced the introduction of conscription. However, fear of a negative nationalist reaction meant that Northern Ireland was not included. Craigavon's demand that the decision be reversed annoyed nationalists and de Valera also voiced his concerns. Craigavon only accepted the decision following a meeting with Chamberlain in May 1939.

To compensate, Northern Ireland was awarded over £6 million in defence contracts. Particularly involved were the Short and Harland aircraft factory and the Harland and Wolff shipyard. This resulted in a fall in unemployment levels during 1939, but it also meant that Belfast could be a target for enemy bombers.

In May 1940, rallies in favour of conscription were held across Northern Ireland; however, the response was not as positive as hoped. Memories of the Battle of the Somme may have contributed to this, as well as the fact that the recruitment drive was led by Sir Basil Brooke.

In the aftermath of the 1941 Belfast Blitz, the British Labour Minister, Ernest Bevin, again raised the possibility of conscription being introduced in Northern Ireland.
● Most nationalists opposed the move.
● Unionist leadership realised that introducing conscription would create more problems than it would solve.
● The Royal Ulster Constabulary (RUC) Inspector-General warned the government that any attempt to introduce conscription could lead to serious public disorder.

Again, London announced that conscription would not be extended to Northern Ireland.

> **What you need to know**
>
> Conscription was a very touchy issue. Make sure that you can explain how different groups saw the matter.

## The war effort in Northern Ireland: complacency?

REVISED

Northern Ireland was not ready for war. Believing that the province was beyond the range of enemy aircraft, appropriate defence measures (both aerial and ground-based) were not put in place by Stormont.

It was not until well into 1941 that most of the province was covered by **radar** and steps had been taken to establish anti-aircraft batteries. Even then some feared that enemy planes would still not be picked up; others felt that far too few anti-aircraft guns, night-fighters and searchlights were in place.

> **What you need to know**
>
> Northern Ireland played a significant part in the United Kingdom's war effort. It is important that you can explain to examiners what Northern Ireland did – as well as identifying the areas where much more could have been achieved.

# Northern Ireland's industrial, agricultural, military and strategic contributions to the war

Northern Ireland made a large contribution to the war.

## Military service

- Close to 40,000 people joined one of the services. Just over 10 per cent died. It is probable that more of the unionist population would have joined up, but they were employed in **reserved occupations**.
- Many of those who joined up served with considerable distinction.
- Over 43,000 Irish citizens fought for the Allies; however, poor Anglo-Irish relations meant that their contribution was not recognised at home.

## The home guard

Fear of Republican infiltration meant that the B Specials formed the core of the **home guard**. Unlike Britain, the force came under the control of the RUC rather than the Army and was seen as a sectarian force.

The home guard spent much of its time counteracting the IRA. Republicans were seen as pro-German and the government introduced **internment** to deal with IRA suspects. IRA activity eventually dropped off.

## Strategic significance

Northern Ireland played a key strategic role in the war. The return of the treaty ports and Éire's declaration of neutrality in 1939 increased Northern Ireland's value. It was further increased after the fall of France in June 1940 as Allied shipping began to go north of Ireland (the so-called **western approaches**).

- Naval bases, such as Lisahally, provided vital support, services and bases for ships involved in the **Battle of the Atlantic**, thus keeping sea lanes open.
- Derry/Londonderry was an important and busy base for service personnel.
- Natural inlets such as Lough Foyle provided refuge from U-boat attack for **merchant shipping** on their trans-Atlantic journeys.
- Local air bases provided much needed cover for **convoys**.
- US forces used Northern Ireland between 1942 and 1944.
- Northern Ireland was also a base for operations in North Africa, Southern Italy and **D-Day**.

## Was Northern Ireland really prepared for enemy attack?

Northern Ireland did not compare well to Great Britain's wide-ranging evacuation and air raid protection schemes, implemented prior to the outbreak of war.

- Stormont introduced an **Air Raid Precautions** Act in 1938; however, it did not make local council provision of civil defence measures compulsory.
- Evacuation of children only began in July 1940 and only 10 per cent of children were evacuated from Belfast.

- **Air Raid Protection (ARP)** wardens, who had the job of enforcing blackouts, were not taken seriously and blackouts were routinely ignored.
- When people were offered the chance to be evacuated from Belfast, few did so.
- When Belfast was bombed in 1941 there weren't enough recruits for the civil defence services.
- The majority of people did not carry gas masks until after the Belfast Blitz.
- Nearly a year after the declaration of war, only 15 per cent of the Belfast households entitled to an **Anderson air raid shelter** had received one.

## Agriculture

Agriculture was the best-performing section of the economy.
- The amount of land used for growing crops increased by 60 per cent. Particularly significant were the increases in the production of flax, oats and potatoes.
- Allotments increased fourfold
- There were significant increases in cattle and poultry numbers.
- Northern Ireland exported essential sheep, cattle, eggs and dairy produce.

There were two main reasons for this remarkable performance:
- continued availability of fertilisers
- the more than one hundred fold increase in tractor numbers.

Much of the credit for the success of the agricultural sector belongs to the Minister for Agriculture, Basil Brooke. His success was key to his appointment as Prime Minister in 1943.

---

## Revision tasks

TESTED ☐

1 Create a spider diagram on conscription showing:
   - those in favour – and why
   - those against – and why.
2 Write revision notes on Northern Ireland's war efforts using the following headings:
   - Military service
   - The home guard
   - Readiness for attack
3 Create a spider diagram showing the key aspects of Northern Ireland's strategic importance to the Allies.

---

Exam practice answers at **www.hoddereducation.co.uk/myrevisionnotesdownloads**

## Rationing

Rationing was introduced for a number of items including fresh meat, dairy produce and fuel. For some, particularly those close to the border, smuggling eased the shortages; others resorted to the black market.

## Industry

For the first two years of the war industrial output was hit by:
- bad management
- a lack of planning (by early 1941 no new factories had been built)
- a shortage of skilled workers coupled with poor working practices
- a series of strikes (even though they were supposed to be illegal).

It was 1943 before output really improved. Unemployment dropped, production figures climbed and wages and living standards improved. A variety of firms (including Harland & Wolff and Short & Harland) produced a significant number of tanks, ships, aircraft and munitions.

Other companies produced wartime essentials including weapons and ammunition, nets and ropes, uniforms and parachutes. At the same time, some historians argue that Northern Ireland's economic performance should have been better.

**Revision tasks**

1 Examine Northern Ireland's agricultural performance using the following headings:
  - Examples of improvement
  - Reasons for improvement
2 What impact did rationing have on Northern Ireland?
3 Examine Northern Ireland's industrial performance under the headings of:
  - Areas of success
  - Areas of failure

TESTED

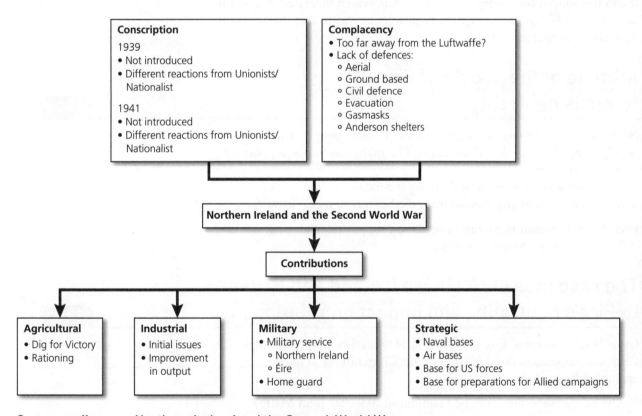

**Summary diagram: Northern Ireland and the Second World War**

# 5 Éire's neutrality and its impact on relationships during the war

## The reasons for de Valera's policy of neutrality

The day after Britain declared war on Germany, de Valera announced Éire's neutrality.

There were a number of reasons for this:
- De Valera correctly assumed that the population would support it to reinforce Éire's independence
- partition ruled out Éire's involvement in the war
- the population was divided over whether or not to support Britain
- many believed Germany posed no threat; if there was a threat, they believed that Britain would protect Éire
- Éire was not equipped to fight a war
- the government wanted to protect its people against the hardships of war.

It also introduced the Emergency Powers Act, which increased its control over the country and gave it extensive powers to ensure that the policy of neutrality was maintained.

> **What you need to know**
>
> Éire's declaration of neutrality is a key element of this course. Are you able to explain why it happened and what the reaction was (within Ireland – and across the British Isles)?

## Attitude of the people of Éire towards neutrality

Neutrality was a popular policy, even though many people remained largely sympathetic to the Allied cause. The main reasons for support for neutrality included:
- belief that it reinforced Ireland's independence
- hope that it might save Ireland from the horrors of modern warfare.

Even Ireland's minority unionist population supported neutrality, while still supporting the Allied war effort.

## The response of Northern Ireland and Britain to Éire's neutrality, and impact on relations

Great Britain accepted Éire's declaration of neutrality only grudgingly. Particular opposition came from Winston Churchill, soon to be appointed Prime Minister.

Realising the importance of good communication, Sir John Maffey was appointed as the British government's representative to Éire. He developed a positive relationship with de Valera. However, Britain never recognised Éire's neutrality and pressure to end the policy remained strong, particularly after Churchill became Prime Minister in May 1940.

There was strong resentment at Éire's neutrality in Northern Ireland; it was viewed as an act of betrayal and a threat to the United Kingdom's security.

# Benevolent neutrality

Éire asserted neutrality as follows:
- it refused military assistance to both sides
- the Allies were denied the use of ports and airfields
- news bulletins gave purely factual reports about the war
- weather forecasts ceased to be broadcast in case they helped either side
- when the USA entered the war, de Valera resisted US pressure to end neutrality.

**What you need to know**

You need to be able to show examiners that you understand what neutrality meant in real terms.

De Valera went to great lengths to appear neutral. He irritated Washington by protesting at the arrival of US troops in Northern Ireland. He annoyed Allied opinion when he expressed sympathy over Hitler's death. However, he had also expressed sympathy at the death of the President, Franklin Delano Roosevelt.

Frequently Dublin's actions made it seem that its neutrality was pro-Allies:
- the German ambassador's radio transmitter was confiscated
- German pilots who bailed out over Éire were imprisoned; Allied airmen were allowed to cross the border into Northern Ireland
- during the Belfast Blitz, de Valera sent fire engines to help. In its aftermath, relief centres were set up close to the border and relief funds were started
- Allied airmen patrolling the western approaches or refuelling on trans-Atlantic missions could fly over Irish territory via the 'Donegal air corridor'
- coastal navigational aids were provided for US airmen
- in the final months of the war, de Valera allowed the RAF to establish secret radar bases in Éire.

It is important to consider the real reasons for Éire's ability to remain neutral.
- Éire benefited from the sympathetic attitude of the British and German representatives in Dublin.
- If the Allies had needed to invade the South they would have done so. That they did not was due to Northern Ireland's significant strategic role.

## Revision tasks

1 Create a spider diagram that shows the reasons for neutrality.
2 Complete the following table with regard to neutrality:

| Irish response | |
| --- | --- |
| British response | |
| Northern Irish response | |

3 Create a spider diagram showing how Éire's neutrality was biased towards the Allies.
4 Can you explain why Éire was able to maintain its neutrality?

# Reaction to Britain's offer to end partition

Britain made two main attempts to encourage Ireland onto her side.

1 In June 1940, London proposed reunification if Éire joined the Allies. In return Dublin would allow British forces to be stationed in Éire and use naval facilities. De Valera rejected the offer due to:
   ○ Éire's 'unpreparedness'
   ○ the negative impact it would have on independence
   ○ the fact that there was no guarantee that Northern Ireland would agree as its government had not been consulted.

2 Following the Japanese attack on Pearl Harbor (7 December 1941), Churchill telegrammed de Valera. His offer of 'Now is your chance. Now or never "A nation once again"', was understood by de Valera to refer to the possibility of Irish unity if he joined the Allies. Again he declined.

In 1942 Churchill attempted to regain the use of the treaty ports. Once again his efforts were rejected.

> **What you need to know**
>
> The ending of partition was referred to more than once during the war. Make sure that you can identify when this happened and what Dublin's reaction was.

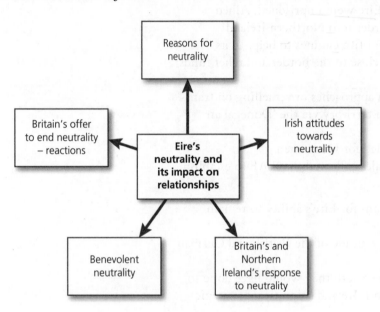

**Summary diagram:** Éire's neutrality and its impact on relationships

# 6 German attacks and their impact on Britain, Northern Ireland and Éire

## The Battle of Britain

REVISED

By the end of June 1940, Britain stood alone against Germany. The army lacked the numbers and equipment needed to defend from invasion, so:
- factories worked multiple shifts to produce aircraft, tanks and heavy weapons. Their efforts were boosted by the introduction of a government campaign for scrap metal
- over 500,000 rifles were ordered from the USA
- the Local Defence Volunteers (later **home guard**) was established in May 1940. In just over a year it had over a million members.

> **What you need to know**
>
> The Battle of Britain was probably a key turning point in the war. Can you explain why it happened – and why it was so very important?

Although the Royal Navy had begun a blockade of the North Sea and was patrolling the Channel to defend against the German Navy, the RAF was in a stronger position than other branches of the military. Radar provided advance warning of the approach of enemy aircraft while the RAF was reorganised into three sections: Fighter Command, Bomber Command and Coastal Command.

## The events of the Battle

In July 1940, Britain rejected Hitler's offer of a peaceful end to the war in return for Britain recognising Nazi domination of Western Europe. Hitler then implemented Operation Sealion, the invasion of Britain by sea. Before this could start the RAF would have to be destroyed.

**Table 3.2 The events of the Battle of Britain**

| Date | Event |
|---|---|
| 12 August 1940 | The *Luftwaffe* launched Operation Eagle, its attack on the RAF. This included:<br>• bombing RAF airfields and destroying planes on the ground<br>• shooting down any planes that were able to take off.<br><br>Although initial *Luftwaffe* losses were greater, it had significantly more aircraft and so it is likely that if these attacks had continued the RAF would eventually have been worn down. |
| 7 September 1940 | The *Luftwaffe* switched tactics in response to recent RAF raids on Berlin and started to bomb London. The raids continued for months and were extended to include cities such as Coventry, Liverpool and Glasgow.<br><br>While the nightly blitz caused massive devastation, the change of *Luftwaffe* tactics allowed the RAF to reorganise and obtain newly manufactured aircraft. |
| 17 September 1940 | Operation Sealion was called off. |

## The significance of the Battle of Britain

The Battle of Britain was significant for a number of reasons:
- it was the first important military campaign to be fought entirely by aircraft, showing how technology was changing the nature of war
- it was the largest and most continuous aerial bombing campaign to have been undertaken
- it was the first defeat of Germany's forces since the start of the Second World War. The German leader now made the decision to switch his attention to the invasion of the USSR, a decision that would ultimately play a significant part in the defeat of the Nazis
- it was a significant morale boost to the people of Great Britain, reinforcing their decision to keep going in their fight against Germany.

## MacDermott's Reforms

In June 1940 John MacDermott was appointed as Northern Ireland's Minister of Public Security. He organised:

- the rapid erection of public air raid shelters
- the reinforcement of the emergency services
- efforts to evacuate children from Belfast.

In addition, blackout curtains were used to stop lights showing the *Luftwaffe* the locations of towns and cities.

**Revision tasks**

1 Make notes showing the steps that Britain took to prepare for war.
2 Analyse the Battle of Britain using the following headings:
   - Background
   - Events
   - Outcome
3 Create a spider diagram showing the reforms introduced by John MacDermott after June 1940.

TESTED ☐

REVISED ☐

## The events of the Belfast *Blitz*

When the *Luftwaffe* bombed Belfast in April and May 1941, the city still only had 22 anti-aircraft guns, insufficient air cover from fighter aircraft and public shelters capable of housing no more than a quarter of the population.

The *Luftwaffe* bombed Belfast four times (7–8 April, 15–16 April, 4–5 May and 5–6 May) for a number of reasons:

- the key role that some of the city's industries were playing in the war effort
- Northern Ireland's strategic importance.

As a result:

- 955 civilians were killed and 2436 injured
- almost 57,000 homes were damaged or destroyed, leaving thousands homeless
- thousands fled Belfast to the rest of Northern Ireland and even to Éire, enduring harsh conditions
- Belfast's industrial infrastructure suffered extensive damage. It took six months for industrial production to recover.

**What you need to know**

When discussing the impact of the Second World War everyone considers the *Blitz*. Make sure that you are able to write about the reasons for, details of and impact of *Luftwaffe* bombing raids on Belfast – and other parts of Northern Ireland and Éire.

## The impact of the *Luftwaffe* raids

REVISED ☐

Relatively speaking, Belfast suffered more from *Luftwaffe* attacks than other British cities had up to that point. The 745 deaths that resulted from the raid of 15–16 April was greater than the deaths resulting from a single raid elsewhere in the United Kingdom.

Other parts of Northern Ireland also suffered, including Derry/Londonderry, Bangor and Newtownards.

The attacks also exposed the poverty, poor quality of housing and poor health in Northern Ireland, particularly in urban areas.

- Massive improvements to housing were needed, alongside a substantial programme of house building and improvements to health and education.
- The foundations for post-war reforms were laid in the destruction caused – and revealed – by the Belfast Blitz. In light of the appalling health of many of its poorest citizens, Stormont established a new Ministry of Health and Local Government in 1944.

**What you need to know**

With regards to the Blitz you need to be able to explain its impact on lives, property and industry.

**Revision tasks**

1 Make notes on the Belfast Blitz using the following headings:
   - Reasons
   - Results
2 Create a spider diagram showing the impact of the Belfast Blitz.

TESTED ☐

# Éire and the Blitz

Despite neutrality, there remained the possibility that Germany might invade Éire before invading Britain. This possibility – discussed by representatives of both governments – also made it likely that British Army units would move into Éire to secure its vulnerable western flanks.

Aware of its limitations, the government increased Éire's military capacity by:
- increasing the size of the army to over 40,000
- creating a reserve force – the Local Defence Force. However, it was poorly equipped
- extending the size of the navy
- establishing an air force.

De Valera also moved against the IRA. Using the Offences against the State Act, internment was implemented against up to 1,000 suspected IRA members. Six IRA members were hanged and when a further three went on hunger strike nothing was done to prevent their deaths. De Valera's stance – which broke the IRA – was supported by the vast majority of the population.

## The effects of the war on Éire

The war – or 'Emergency' as it was called – impacted on Éire as follows:

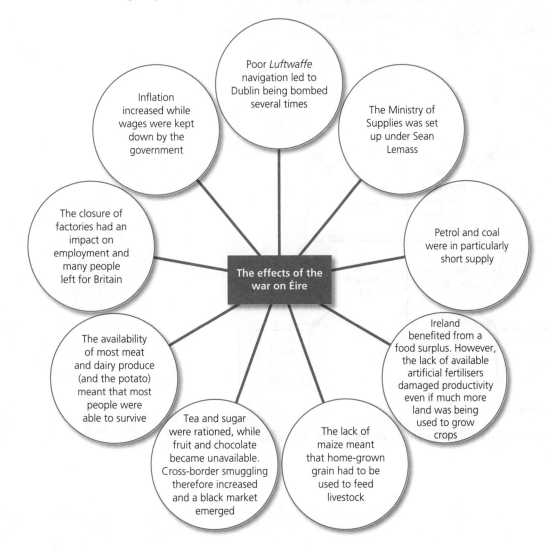

**What you need to know**

The war had a real impact on Éire. Make sure that you can show examiners what this impact was, as well as how the Dublin government responded to it.

Option 1 Changing Relations: Northern Ireland and its Neighbours, 1920–49

However, there were no wartime blackouts in Éire and cinemas and theatres remained open for business – including to patrons from Northern Ireland.

Despite the support for neutrality, harsh conditions meant that *Fianna Fáil* lost ten seats in the 1943 general election. Within a year all but one of these seats had been regained in another election, called by de Valera to take advantage of the increased popularity of his government as a result of the Allies' decision to isolate Ireland in advance of D-Day. This followed de Valera's refusal to close the German and Japanese embassies in Dublin to prevent leaks of the Allied invasion plans.

## Exam practice

2 Study Source B below and answer the question which follows:

### Source B

The two great principles for which so many have died – no partition and no control of Ireland by any foreign power – have gone by the board in this treaty.

> Sean T. O'Kelly provides the view of those members of
> *Sinn Féin* who opposed the Treaty, December 1921.

Using Source B and your contextual knowledge, give two reasons from Source B to explain why some Republicans opposed the 1921 Treaty.　　　　　　　　　　　　[4]

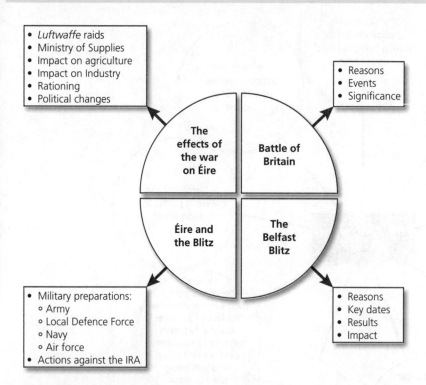

- *Luftwaffe* raids
- Ministry of Supplies
- Impact on agriculture
- Impact on Industry
- Rationing
- Political changes

**The effects of the war on Éire**

**Battle of Britain**

- Reasons
- Events
- Significance

**Éire and the Blitz**

**The Belfast Blitz**

- Military preparations:
  ○ Army
  ○ Local Defence Force
  ○ Navy
  ○ Air force
- Actions against the IRA

- Reasons
- Key dates
- Results
- Impact

**Summary diagram:** German attacks and their impact on Britain, Northern Ireland and Éire

# 7 Life in post-war Northern Ireland and Éire, 1945–49

In May 1945 the Second World War ended in Europe; two months later Clement Attlee's Labour Party won the British general election. Voters were attracted by Labour's promises of jobs for all, government ownership of industry and the introduction of a **Welfare State**.

## The new Labour government's policies in Britain

REVISED

The new government faced a very difficult situation:
- the country was almost broke
- poverty was widespread
- most of the goods being made in Britain were being exported so that food could be imported
- coal, bread and potato supplies had almost run out.

As a result the immediate post-war period in Britain was known as the 'age of austerity'.

Labour's policy of **nationalisation** was implemented as follows:
- 1947: coal mines and electricity
- 1948: railways
- 1949: iron and steel.

The government also began to build houses to eliminate slums and repair the damage caused by the Blitz.

> **What you need to know**
>
> The election of a Labour government in 1945 had a real impact on politics in the United Kingdom. Make sure that you are able to explain fully why it was elected and what the reactions to its election were, especially in Northern Ireland.

## The reaction at Stormont to Labour's victory in Westminster

In the past, the Labour Party had been strongly critical of Northern Ireland. Some unionists were worried about the new government, its plans for social reform and how much it would cost. In the end, however, it was felt that Northern Ireland's best chance of staying economically stable was to keep its close relationship with Great Britain.

## The establishment of the Welfare State in Britain and Northern Ireland

REVISED

The National Health Service (NHS) was introduced in July 1948.
- It faced opposition from those concerned about the costs.
- It faced opposition from doctors fearing that it would limit their careers.
- In the end, the NHS was joined by 90 per cent of doctors.
- It was hugely successful, even if it was massively expensive, and it greatly benefited public health in the UK.

> **What you need to know**
>
> The setting up of the Welfare State is a really important development. Can you explain what it was, why it was established – and what its impact was?

# Reasons for and attitudes to the introduction of the Welfare State in Northern Ireland

The destruction of the Belfast Blitz showed there was an urgent need to look after the poor and sick who lived in slums or in houses that were not fit to be lived in.

Despite the need for massive reforms in health care and housing, many in Northern Ireland's middle classes and medical profession feared what Labour's policies might mean for them. Stormont also feared the loss of power to a centralising socialist government and wondered how it was to finance such reforms.

The less well-off welcomed the Welfare State, while nationalists welcomed the initiative as they saw a Labour government as potentially more sympathetic to their situation.

Stormont need not have worried; Labour showed its gratitude for Northern Ireland's war effort by helping to cover the costs of the introduction of the Welfare State. As a result, improvements were effected in a range of areas.

## The impact of the Welfare State in Northern Ireland

REVISED

The three main areas of reform were the NHS, housing and the economy, as shown in Table 3.3.

**Table 3.3 The three main areas of reform**

| Area of reform | Results |
|----------------|---------|
| The NHS | • The new system began in 1948 and was soon fighting against polio and tuberculosis.<br>• By 1962, Northern Ireland's death rate was the lowest in the UK; in 1939 it had been the highest. |
| Housing | • The Northern Ireland Housing Trust was established in 1945 to oversee the construction of new houses.<br>• Local councils were also encouraged to build houses; however, they were not as successful.<br>• The way in which those council houses were given to people meant that not all benefited equally. |
| The economy | • There had been a long-term decline in some traditional industries, such as linen and shipbuilding.<br>• The 1945 Industrial Development Act incentivised building new factories. |

Northern Ireland was also helped by the introduction of the **family allowance**, **national assistance** and **non-contributing pensions**.

While living standards improved, these reforms meant that Stormont came to rely on the British government for money. This was resented by some unionist politicians.

## Revision tasks

1 Make notes explaining why the post-war years were called the 'age of austerity' and how the Westminster government responded to the problems it was facing.

2 How did Northern Ireland's population react to:
● the election of a Labour government
● the introduction of the Welfare State?

TESTED

## What you need to know

The introduction of the Welfare State was a major development in the history of Great Britain and Northern Ireland. You should be able to explain what changes were introduced and what impact these changes had.

# The 1947 (Northern Ireland) Education Act and its impact

REVISED

The 1947 Education Act introduced radical changes.

- The school-leaving age was raised to 15 (with transfer to post-primary school at the age of 11). Over the following eight years the numbers of students in post-primary education doubled.
- Education authorities had to provide transport, milk, meals, books, stationery and health care to all schools.
- New secondary schools were constructed to cope with the increased numbers in education while funding for the voluntary sector increased to 65 per cent.
- Scholarships were also provided to allow more people to access third-level education.
- Teacher training provision was also improved in both Catholic and Protestant sectors.

These reforms greatly helped the Catholic population. In spite of their poor backgrounds, more Catholic children could now go to secondary schools and universities. However, as the Catholic population became more educated, some of its members began to speak out against what they saw as the inequality and discrimination within Northern Ireland.

> **What you need to know**
>
> Northern Ireland's education system was also reformed; can you outline why this was needed, what changes were introduced – and what the outcome was?

## Exam practice

**3** Study Source C and answer the question which follows:

**Source C**

"On the other hand, it's quite possible his story of taking a wrong turning could be perfectly true."

A cartoon published during the Anglo-Irish Economic War comments humorously on the increase in cross-border smuggling.

How useful is Source C for a historian studying the impact of the Anglo-Irish Economic War on the economies of both parts of Ireland?

Explain your answer, using Source C and your contextual knowledge. [5]

# Exam practice

4 Study Source C again and answer the question below:

How reliable is Source C for a historian studying the reasons for the Economic War and its impact on relations between The Irish Free State, Northern Ireland and Britain?

Explain your answer, using Source C and your contextual knowledge. [6]

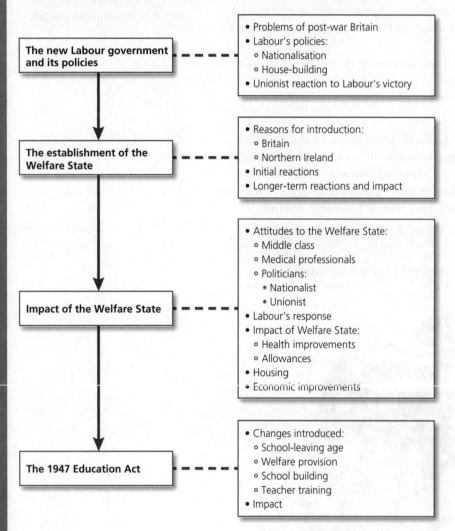

| The new Labour government and its policies | • Problems of post-war Britain<br>• Labour's policies:<br>  ○ Nationalisation<br>  ○ House-building<br>• Unionist reaction to Labour's victory |
| --- | --- |
| The establishment of the Welfare State | • Reasons for introduction:<br>  ○ Britain<br>  ○ Northern Ireland<br>• Initial reactions<br>• Longer-term reactions and impact |
| Impact of the Welfare State | • Attitudes to the Welfare State:<br>  ○ Middle class<br>  ○ Medical professionals<br>  ○ Politicians:<br>    ▪ Nationalist<br>    ▪ Unionist<br>• Labour's response<br>• Impact of Welfare State:<br>  ○ Health improvements<br>  ○ Allowances<br>• Housing<br>• Economic improvements |
| The 1947 Education Act | • Changes introduced:<br>  ○ School-leaving age<br>  ○ Welfare provision<br>  ○ School building<br>  ○ Teacher training<br>• Impact |

**Summary diagram:** Life in post-war Northern Ireland and Éire

# 8 Constitutional changes and effects on relationships

## Social and economic developments in Éire after 1945

REVISED

After 1945, Éire was isolated economically. The result was a severe economic depression:

- unemployment shot up
- building materials became almost unobtainable – so houses could not be built
- the lack of fertilisers limited productivity. Bad weather in 1946–47 further impacted on production
- Britain withheld coal imports
- Éire experienced severe fuel shortages in 1947 due to the weather
- wartime rationing remained in force and was extended to include bread from the start of 1947
- inflation began to rise and a wave of strikes broke out.

Emigration rates remained high, with as many as 24,000 leaving Éire each year.

### A State of Emergency

The situation deteriorated to the point where de Valera declared a State of Emergency. The result was increased unpopularity for the *Fianna Fáil* government and so it lost the 1948 general election and a coalition government took power. It was made up of:

- *Fine Gael* – led by General Richard Mulcahy
- two different Labour parties, each opposed to the other
- *Clann na Talmhan* – representing farmers
- *Clann na Poblachta* – a republican and socialist party led by Seán MacBride (Chief of Staff of the IRA 1936–38).

The new government also had the support of 12 independent TDs.

As leader of the largest party, Mulcahy should have become *Taoiseach*. However, he was unacceptable to MacBride because of his role in the Irish Civil War. Therefore, *Fine Gael's* John A Costello became *Taoiseach*.

The new inter-party government introduced a range of policies to modernise the Irish economy, including:

- the establishment of the Industrial Development Authority (IDA) in 1949 to revitalise the economy
- the creation of *Córas Tráchtála* to increase trade with North America
- a house-building programme which resulted in the building of close to 12,000 new houses annually by 1950
- the start of huge land reclamation projects and the extension of electrification schemes
- the signing of a trade agreement with Britain in 1948. This improved profit margins for Irish agricultural exports.

As a result, the Irish economy entered into a slow but steady period of improvement; however, the failure to start longer-term economic planning meant that the economy did not develop as quickly as it might. At the same time, emigration continued to bleed away the potential of the Irish population.

> **What you need to know**
>
> Post-war Éire was in a bit of a mess and the first change of government in 16 years was a major development. Make sure you can explain why this happened, which parties made up the new administration and what actions it took to make things better.

> **Revision tasks**
>
> 1 Create a spider diagram to illustrate post-war problems in Éire.
> 2 Create a spider diagram that explains the different groups/individuals that made up the inter-party government.
> 3 List the steps that this new government took to try and improve the Irish economy.
>
> TESTED

# Éire's announcement of its intention to become a Republic

REVISED ☐

The members of the inter-party government – particularly *Clann na Poblachta* – felt that the 1937 Constitution had made Éire a republic in all but name. Therefore, in November 1948 the **Republic of Ireland** Bill was introduced, becoming law on Easter Monday 1949.

## Reaction among the people of Northern Ireland to Éire's intention

Reactions were mixed.
- Nationalists unsuccessfully demanded seats in the *Dáil*. Many of them felt abandoned by Dublin and objected to the inter-party government's claim that it represented the whole island.
- Unionists felt threatened. Fearing that the Republic would now try to reunite Ireland, they rejected Dublin's offers of any reasonable **constitutional** guarantees if they were to agree to end partition.

> **What you need to know**
>
> The changes to Éire's constitution are of great significance. Make sure that you are able to explain why these changes were introduced – as well as what impact they had.

# The significance of the Anti-Partition League and the 'chapel gate election'

REVISED ☐

Stormont, therefore, used the border issue as the justification for calling a general election in February 1949.
- Brooke urged unionists to vote for Northern Ireland's continued membership of the UK.
- Nationalists were urged to vote for a united Ireland. It called for the support of its backers in the Republic of Ireland and, as a result, it was agreed to set up an 'anti-partition fund' to help finance the election campaign.

The election became known as the 'chapel gate election' as much of the money used to fund the nationalists' campaign was raised mainly through collections outside churches in the South. This caused great resentment within the unionist community.

The result was an increased share of votes and seats for both unionists and nationalists, with the former still controlling Stormont.

# Declaration of the Republic of Ireland, 1949

REVISED ☐

As Éire was the first country to leave the Commonwealth there was concern about Britain's reaction. However, Australia and Canada supported Éire, stating that there was no reason why an Irish Republic could not continue to work closely with the Commonwealth.

As a consequence, London decided that it would not treat Éire as a foreign country but as a neighbour with a special relationship.

## Reactions and effects, and the impact on relations

The resulting Ireland Act stated that:
- passports were not needed for travel between the two countries
- working permits were not required for Irish workers in the UK or British workers in the Republic of Ireland
- citizens of both nations had voting rights in each other's elections – if they were living in the other country
- Éire would continue to enjoy preferential treatment regarding trade.

Exam practice answers at **www.hoddereducation.co.uk/myrevisionnotesdownloads**

The Act also stated that the Northern Ireland Parliament had been given the final word in any future debate about the ending of partition. As a result:

- Unionists were reassured by these guarantees. Their control of Northern Ireland was confirmed and partition made much more difficult to end. Relations between the Belfast and London governments did not deteriorate as much as might initially have been expected.
- Dublin and Northern Ireland's nationalists were outraged and strongly expressed their displeasure with the Act, particularly the guarantees regarding partition.

Dublin's foreign policy focus became persuading London to remove the border. However, nothing was changed; Attlee felt that, as Dublin had not consulted him about the declaration of the Republic, he was free to give whatever guarantees he wanted to Northern Ireland.

## Exam practice

5 a Name the Northern Irish Prime Minister appointed in 1943. [1]
  b Give one reason for de Valera's declaration of neutrality in 1939. [1]
  c Name one section of the reorganised RAF. [1]
  d Describe one reason why doctors opposed the introduction of the Welfare State. [2]
6 Explain two of the following:
  A The effects of the war on Éire
  B The reasons for the 1937 Constitution
  C The different reactions to the 1920 Government of Ireland Act

  Explanation One: (A, B or C)

  Explanation Two: (B or C if you chose A; A or B if you chose C; A or C if you chose B) [9+9]

- British and Commonwealth reactions
- Ireland Act:
  - Continued rights
  - Guarantee for Northern Ireland
- Reactions to guarantee:
  - Unionists
  - Nationalists
  - Dublin

- Economic problems:
  - Unemployment
  - Lack of materials
  - Lack of fertilisers
  - Fuel shortages
  - Rationing
  - Inflation
  - Emigration
  - State of Emergency

**Reactions: Britain and the Commonwealth**

**Post-war problems**

**Declaration of a Republic and Northern Ireland**

**The inter-party government**

- Republic of Ireland Act:
  - Reasons
- Ireland declared a republic:
  - Unionist reactions
  - Nationalist reactions
- 'Chapel Gate Election':
  - Unionist campaign
  - Nationalist campaign

- 1948 election:
  - Different parties/ individuals
  - Costello as *Taoiseach*
- New policies:
  - IDA
  - *Córas Tráchtála*
  - House-building
  - Rend reclamation
  - Trade Agreement
- Continued emigration

**Summary diagram:** Constitutional changes and effects on relationships

# Option 2 Changing Relations: Northern Ireland and its Neighbours 1965–98

## Introduction

REVISED

Northern Ireland was established by the 1920 Government of Ireland Act. This Act partitioned Ireland into two parts:

- a 26-county Southern Ireland (which later became the Irish Free State)
- a six-county Northern Ireland.

The population of Northern Ireland reacted to the new arrangements differently.

- Unionists – mostly Protestants – were delighted. The new state had a substantial Protestant majority guaranteeing their control. In the May 1921 elections, unionists won 40 out of the 52 seats available.
- Nationalists – mostly Catholics – were deeply upset; they wanted to be governed by a parliament in Dublin.

> **What you need to know**
>
> This is background information which you will not be asked about directly in the examination. However, this detail will help you understand why problems began to emerge in the 1960s.

## Violence and discrimination

Most unionists felt that nationalists could not be trusted and in this atmosphere the number of sectarian killings rocketed. The new government:

- passed the Special Powers Act (1922), allowing it to arrest and detain suspects without trial
- abolished Proportional Representation (PR) for local elections. This meant that fewer nationalists would be elected to councils
- re-drew local council boundaries to ensure unionist control even where there was a nationalist majority. This was known as **gerrymandering**
- allowed only those who paid rates to vote in local elections. This usually resulted in extra votes for the wealthy – who tended to be Protestant – and no votes for the poor – who were mostly, but not always, Catholic.

Discrimination was also practised against Catholics in other ways:

- Catholics were given fewer houses than Protestants by the unionist-controlled councils since ownership of a house gave a vote in local elections
- the quality of much Catholic housing was inferior
- Catholics were less likely to have a job than Protestants.

## Developments up to 1963

The political, economic and social conditions created in the early 1920s remained largely unchanged until the 1960s, although in the late 1940s the Welfare State was introduced to improve living conditions.

However, relations with the South (the Republic of Ireland since 1949) remained tense, particularly as Articles II and III of its 1937 constitution laid claim to the whole of the island. Furthermore, an IRA campaign in opposition to the border (1956–62) reinforced the unionist view that nationalists were untrustworthy. This was despite the fact that the campaign actually failed due to a lack of nationalist support.

# 1 The O'Neill years

## O'Neill's policies and actions

REVISED

In March 1963, Captain Terence O'Neill became Prime Minister of Northern Ireland. O'Neill's position was weak from the start as most of the Official Unionist Party's (OUP) MPs had wanted another minister, Brian Faulkner, to get the job. However, at that time the OUP leader was decided by a group of senior party members, not by election.

O'Neill's main concern lay with improving the economy. Therefore he proposed and introduced many improvements:

- £900 million investment and the creation of five economic zones to update existing industries and attract new ones
- modernisation of the road and railway network
- co-operation with the Dublin-based Irish Trades Union Congress, whose support was important for economic development
- the establishment of an Economic Council to drive forward the modernisation of the economy
- the creation of a Ministry of Development to drive economic revival
- the establishment of a new city called Craigavon
- the development of a new university in Coleraine to help develop a skilled workforce.

**What you need to know**

You should be able to explain why O'Neill wanted to improve the economy, how he went about doing this and what the results of his policies were.

**Table 4.1 Successes and failures of O'Neill's policies and actions**

| Successes of O'Neill's policies and actions | Failures of O'Neill's policies and actions |
|---|---|
| <ul><li>Over 35,000 new jobs were created during the 1960s.</li><li>Multinational firms such as Michelin and DuPont, opened factories in Northern Ireland.</li><li>Motorway construction began.</li><li>An oil refinery was opened in Belfast.</li><li>A new airport was under development.</li><li>Links with the Republic of Ireland resulted in the signing of an agreement on the supply of electricity from south of the border.</li></ul> | <ul><li>Over 20,000 jobs were lost in traditional industries such as linen manufacture.</li><li>The government had to give money to shipbuilders Harland & Wolff.</li><li>Unemployment averaged between seven and eight per cent.</li><li>Several companies refused grants to open factories west of the River Bann, seeing the area as too far from their export markets.</li></ul> |

The lack of investment in the west not only impacted on unemployment levels (over 12.5 per cent in the west) but also fed allegations of bias in government policy as the majority of the population in the west was nationalist.

## Revision tasks

TESTED

1 Create a spider diagram illustrating O'Neill's economic policies.
2 Analyse O'Neill's economic policies using the headings:
- Areas of success
- Areas of failure

# O'Neill's attempts to improve community relations in Northern Ireland

Within Northern Ireland O'Neill tried to improve relations with nationalists by:
- visiting Cardinal William Conway
- offering official condolences when Pope John XXIII died in June 1963
- visiting Catholic schools and hospitals
- increasing financial support for Catholic hospitals and schools.

On the whole, these actions were appreciated by Northern Ireland's nationalist community.

> **What you need to know**
>
> It is important that you can explain why O'Neill wanted to improve relations within Northern Ireland and how he went about doing so.

# O'Neill's attempts to improve relations with the Republic of Ireland

O'Neill met *Taoiseach* Seán Lemass twice in January 1965, first at Stormont and then in Dublin. In both meetings, discussions centered on economic co-operation rather than political issues.

> **What you need to know**
>
> Relations with the Republic of Ireland had been poor for many years. O'Neill wanted to change this; can you explain how he tried to do this – and whether or not he was successful?

## The emergence of Reverend Ian Paisley

There was both support and opposition within the unionist community for O'Neill's attempts to change Northern Ireland. In the short term, he enjoyed increased support from unionists: in the November 1965 general election the OUP won 38 out of 52 seats.

However, evidence of the divisions within the OUP over the visit of Lemass became clear when Brian Faulkner condemned O'Neill's failure to consult his cabinet.

While there was no widespread hostile public reaction to Lemass' visit, Reverend Ian Paisley, **Moderator** of the Free Presbyterian Church, strongly objected because of:
- the great influence of the Catholic Church in the South
- the claims to the whole of the island, laid out it in Articles II and III of the Republic's constitution.

## Violence and division

Tensions increased in 1966 with the 50th anniversary commemorations of the Easter Rising and the Battle of the Somme. Rioting broke out. Then two Catholics died in May and June 1966, the result of gun attacks by the re-emerging UVF. O'Neill responded by banning the organisation.

OUP divisions increased and support from the unionist population continued to decrease through the late 1960s.
- There was a plot among backbench MPs in late 1966 to remove O'Neill as leader.
- Rumours emerged of opposition from key ministers Brian Faulkner and Harry West.
- Opinion polls showed reduced support for O'Neill and increased support for Paisley.

# Nationalist reactions: satisfaction and disappointment

Initially, Catholic leaders reacted positively to O'Neill's policies and actions. The nationalist Party took up the role of official opposition in Stormont for the first time in history, following Lemass' visit.

However, O'Neill's policies also raised expectations, some of which were unlikely to be met given the growing tensions within Unionism. Annoyance was particularly felt among a new generation of Catholics at:

- the decision to name the new city linking Portadown and Lurgan, Craigavon, after Northern Ireland's first Prime Minister
- O'Neill's economic policies favouring the Protestant east
- no significant attempts being made to increase Catholic membership of various health and education bodies.

## Revision tasks

TESTED ☐

1 Create a spider diagram showing the steps that O'Neill introduced to improve relations with nationalists.
2 Analyse unionist reactions to O'Neill's policies under the following headings:
   - Evidence of support
   - Evidence of opposition from within the OUP
   - Reverend Ian Paisley
   - UVF
3 Create a spider diagram to illustrate the evidence put forward by nationalists to suggest O'Neill's reforms were biased against them.

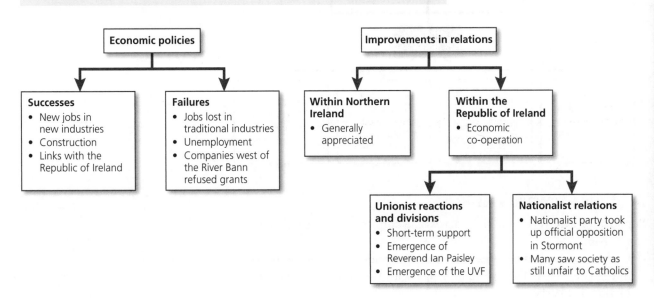

**Summary diagram:** The O'Neill years

# 2 The campaign for civil rights

## The influence of the civil rights movement in the USA

REVISED

The success of the US **civil rights** movement was widely known in Europe.
- Martin Luther King Jr's campaign had used non-violent methods of **civil disobedience** to achieve equal opportunities for black people.
- By 1967 a series of marches and protests had led the US Congress to pass laws outlawing public discrimination and guaranteeing voting rights.

Inspired by these successes, the Northern Ireland Civil Rights Association (NICRA) was established at the start of 1967. At the same time there were other sources of encouragement in the period following NICRA's establishment, notably the student demonstrations that took place in France during 1968.

**What you need to know**

You should know all of the key points about NICRA's origins, aims and tactics – and about the reactions to them.

## Reasons for the emergence of NICRA

REVISED

Set up as a non-sectarian movement, NICRA did not seek to end partition. Its goals were:

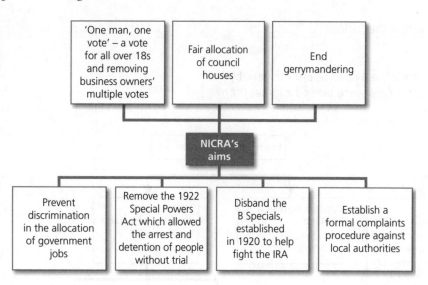

'One man, one vote' – a vote for all over 18s and removing business owners' multiple votes

Fair allocation of council houses

End gerrymandering

**NICRA's aims**

Prevent discrimination in the allocation of government jobs

Remove the 1922 Special Powers Act which allowed the arrest and detention of people without trial

Disband the B Specials, established in 1920 to help fight the IRA

Establish a formal complaints procedure against local authorities

## Attitudes towards NICRA

Support for NICRA came from across the community. In particular it came from:
- Catholics who had benefited from the introduction of free education in the late 1940s. They were unhappy with the performance of the Nationalist Party
- **Liberal** Protestants who supported some NICRA demands and believed that making Northern Ireland fairer would undermine demands for a United Ireland
- other groups and individuals including communists, academics and trade unionists.

At the same time there was suspicion from within the unionist population. Some felt NICRA:

● was intent on causing trouble and was just a front for the IRA
● was only interested in Catholic rights and would undermine the position of Protestants
● wanted a united Ireland, thus threatening the continued existence of Northern Ireland.

## Early civil rights marches and responses

REVISED

NICRA's first march was held on 24 August 1968 between Coalisland and Dungannon. The event – which sought to highlight inequalities in council house allocation – passed off without incident.

To highlight inequalities in Londonderry **Corporation**'s housing policy, a march was organised for 5 October.

● In response, the unionist **apprentice boys** threatened to hold a rival march.
● The government responded by banning all marches; NICRA rejected this ban.
● While relatively few marchers turned up, they were joined by four Westminster MPs and an RTE camera crew which recorded and then broadcast the RUC's heavy-handed efforts to stop the march.

Further NICRA marches made the situation even worse. Quite often violence resulted.

### The Five-Point Reform Programme

O'Neill, Faulkner and Craig were summoned on 4 November to meet the British Labour Prime Minister Harold Wilson to discuss the unrest in Northern Ireland. These talks resulted in the Five-Point Reform Programme:

1 The allocation of council housing on a **points system**.
2 The replacement of Londonderry Corporation by a Development Commission.
3 The removal of parts of the 1922 Special Powers Act.
4 Local government reforms, including the ending of extra votes for business owners.
5 The appointment of an **ombudsman** to investigate complaints.

Protests and counter-protests continued and on 9 December O'Neill appeared on television. He asked NICRA to help restore calm. This became known as the 'Ulster at the Crossroads' speech.

At first his message seemed to work and NICRA protests were called off. However, there were other problems.

● The reforms dismayed unionists who opposed concessions to the threat of violence and who now felt that their position was under threat.
● O'Neill faced further opposition from within his own party with Home Affairs Minister William Craig condemning his television speech. Craig was sacked, but this did not deter opposition.

**What you need to know**

Examiners will expect you to be able to write about NICRA's early marches, the response to them and about the Five-Point Reform Programme.

**Revision tasks**

1 Analyse NICRA using the following headings:
   ● Date set up
   ● Sources of inspiration
   ● Tactics
   ● Attitude to partition
2 Create a spider diagram to show NICRA's aims.
3 Draw up a table showing who supported NICRA and who did not.
4 Examine NICRA's early marches using the headings:
   ● Date and location
   ● Reasons
   ● Outcome
5 Create a spider diagram explaining the Five-Point Reform Programme.
6 Analyse O'Neill's television appearance using the following headings:
   ● Background
   ● Impact
   ● Divisions within Unionism

TESTED

# The effectiveness of NICRA and reasons for the emergence of the People's Democracy

REVISED

The announcement of the Five-Point Reform Programme suggests that some of NICRA's aims had been fully – or partially – achieved by the end of 1968. However, not all were satisfied.

NICRA's decision to stop marching was ignored by the recently formed People's Democracy. This group, made up mainly of university students, had emerged out of anger at the violence NICRA had faced in October 1968. Its leading figures were Michael Farrell and Bernadette Devlin and its demands were broadly similar to NICRA's:

- one man, one vote
- fair boundaries
- houses on need
- jobs on merit
- free speech
- repeal of the Special Powers Act.

People's Democracy announced a march between Belfast and Derry/Londonderry to show dissatisfaction with the limits of the Five-Point Reform Programme. The march – held in early January 1969 – was condemned by NICRA and nationalist leaders, fearing its impact on an already tense situation. These condemnations were ignored.

> **What you need to know**
>
> Can you explain why the People's Democracy was set up, what its aims were – and what happened as a result of its January 1969 march?

## Ambush at Burntollet

As much of the march was to go through Protestant areas, the police tried to avoid confrontation. However, the march was the target of a violent ambush at Burntollet Bridge, an attack that the police seemed to do little to stop. Then, tensions were further raised in Derry/Londonderry when police rampaged through nationalist areas of the city.

In reaction NICRA started to march again. The first march was held in Newry; again, violence resulted. In response, O'Neill set up the Cameron Commission. This led two cabinet members (including Brian Faulkner) to resign. Faulkner argued that O'Neill was too weak to control the situation.

Then 12 OUP MPs demanded O'Neill's resignation. Instead he called an election – the 'Crossroads Election' – to show he had public support for his policies.

## Reasons for the downfall of O'Neill

REVISED

As a result of the election, held on 24 February 1969:
- there was a reduction in unionist support and divisions of loyalty among the OUP MPs elected
- there was little or no evidence of the hoped-for support from Catholic voters
- O'Neill polled only 1,400 votes more than his opponent, Reverend Ian Paisley.

> **What you need to know**
>
> This is fairly simple – can you explain why O'Neill decided to resign in April 1969?

O'Neill finally resigned on 28 April 1969. This followed a series of bombings, which appeared to be the work of the IRA but which were actually carried out by **loyalists** in an attempt to force O'Neill out. He was succeeded by Major James Chichester Clark.

## Exam practice

1 Study Source A below and answer the question which follows:

### Source A

[Lemass] suddenly said, 'I shall get into terrible trouble for this'. 'No, Mr Lemass,' I replied, 'it is I who will get into trouble for this.'

Terence O'Neill reflecting on the likely impact of his meeting with *Taoiseach* Sean Lemass in his autobiography, *Ulster at the Crossroads* (1969)

Using Source A and your contextual knowledge, give one reason that explains why O'Neill decided to meet with Lemass in 1965. [2]

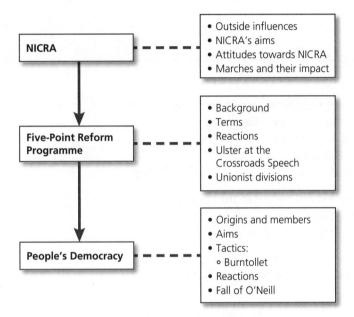

**NICRA**
- Outside influences
- NICRA's aims
- Attitudes towards NICRA
- Marches and their impact

**Five-Point Reform Programme**
- Background
- Terms
- Reactions
- Ulster at the Crossroads Speech
- Unionist divisions

**People's Democracy**
- Origins and members
- Aims
- Tactics:
  ○ Burntollet
- Reactions
- Fall of O'Neill

**Summary diagram:** The campaign for civil rights

# 3 A deteriorating situation, 1969–72

## Increasing tensions and violence, summer 1969

REVISED

Post-Burntollet civil rights protests became more confrontational and were followed by serious rioting in Belfast. As the July–August **marching season** approached:

- Stormont was worried that the security forces would not be able to cope with more violence
- London had established a cabinet committee on Northern Ireland
- Dublin had sent an intelligence officer to Northern Ireland to watch what was happening
- loyalist and republican armed groups seemed to be emerging.

### A long hot summer

- Sectarian violence broke out in Belfast in July.
- In Derry/Londonderry rioting began following the annual apprentice boys parade on 12 August. In total, the rioting during what became known as the Battle of the Bogside lasted for 50 hours. Finally, calm was restored by using a small number of British troops.
- Violence continued elsewhere, especially Belfast.

In the middle of this violence, *Taoiseach* Jack Lynch expressed his concerns at the deteriorating situation. His statement, and the movement of Irish troops and field hospitals to the border, did little to ease tension.

The events of August 1969 were later seen as directly responsible for:

- the deployment of the British Army on the streets of Northern Ireland in an attempt to restore law and order
- the eventual re-emergence of the IRA.

## The reasons for and consequences of the intervention of the Irish and British governments

REVISED

Using the Army might help to stop violence, but new political ideas were also needed. On 19 August, therefore, Chichester Clark met Harold Wilson. The outcome was the Downing Street Declaration. This aimed to reassure both communities.

- Nationalists were told that 'every citizen of Northern Ireland is entitled to the same equality of treatment and freedom from discrimination as [exists] in the rest of the UK irrespective of political views or religion'.
- Unionists were told that 'Northern Ireland should not cease to be part of the UK without the consent of the people of Northern Ireland'.

> **What you need to know**
>
> The political situation really began to deteriorate from mid-1969 onwards; make sure you are able to explain why.

> **What you need to know**
>
> The **Downing Street Declaration** was a key development – examiners will want you to be able to explain what its main terms were and how people responded to them.

## Additional reforms

Further reforms were announced or introduced in the following weeks:
● one man, one vote and an end to gerrymandering
● a committee on policing, chaired by Lord Hunt
● a **tribunal** to investigate recent disturbances, led by Lord Scarman
● a single housing authority to take over housing functions from local councils
● measures to prevent discrimination in public employment
● the creation of a Ministry of Community Relations.

There were also moves to improve the economy:
● a £2 million programme of job-creating schemes
● increases in investment grants.

Despite the reassurances of the Declaration, many unionists were concerned at continuing concessions to nationalists. The final straw came when the Hunt Report was published. It recommended:
● disarming the RUC
● disbanding the B Specials and replacing them with the Ulster Defence Regiment.

Angered at the proposals, violence erupted on Belfast's Shankill Road. Nationalists, however, reacted positively to the reforms, believing that an improved future was now within their grasp.

## The re-emergence of the Irish Republican Army (IRA), the split in the IRA and the objectives of the newly-formed Provisional IRA

REVISED

Since the ending of its 1962 border campaign, the IRA had become more interested in **Marxism**. However, some of its younger members wanted to take matters into their own hands, particularly the defence of nationalist areas.

### The split in the IRA and the objectives of the Provisional IRA

In late 1969 the IRA split into:
● the Official IRA (OIRA); it continued to focus on establishing a Marxist Ireland. Violence was still used until a ceasefire in May 1972. In 1974 the movement split again with the emergence of the Irish Republican Socialist Party (IRSP) and – in 1975 – the militant Irish Nationalist Liberation Army (INLA).
● the Provisional IRA (PIRA).

By Easter 1970, PIRA had stated its objectives:
● civil rights
● defence of the Catholic population
● the destruction of the Stormont government
● the removal of 'British **imperialism**' from Ireland.

## Revision tasks

1 Analyse the People's Democracy march using the headings:
   ● Reasons
   ● Events
   ● Results
2 When and why did O'Neill resign; who replaced him?
3 Analyse the Downing Street Declaration using the following headings:
   ● Background
   ● Key terms
   ● Reforms introduced
   ● Reactions
4 How did unionists and nationalists react to these reforms?

TESTED

### What you need to know

The split within the IRA and nationalist attitudes to the British Army are key issues. You need to be able to explain the key details and the political implications of these developments.

## PIRA and the British Army

PIRA's campaign – which took off in the middle of 1970 – placed the British Army in a difficult position. On its arrival the Army had been welcomed by most nationalists.

## The Falls Road curfew

The Army felt it had to respond to the growing PIRA threat. In July 1970 it imposed a 36-hour curfew on the Lower Falls area of Belfast during a house-to-house search for weapons. Although some weapons, ammunition and explosives were discovered, the search badly damaged the Army's relationship with the nationalist community and helped increase PIRA membership.

# The re-emergence of the Ulster Volunteer Force (UVF) and its objectives, and the setting up of the Ulster Defence Association (UDA)

REVISED

Protestant paramilitaries also wanted to see an end to the Stormont regime.
- They wanted a return to unionist domination.
- The UVF had re-emerged in the mid-1960s and had grown against the background of NICRA's campaign and what was seen as O'Neill's **appeasement** of Catholics.
- It sought to oppose Republican paramilitaries and ensure that Northern Ireland remained a part of the United Kingdom.
- September 1971 saw the formation of the Ulster Defence Association (UDA). It saw itself as protecting Protestant areas and resisting Republican aggression. It was seen as too large to ban. Within the UDA a group known as the Ulster Freedom Fighters (UFF) existed. Its members carried out paramilitary attacks and it was outlawed in 1973.

> **What you need to know**
>
> As with the re-emergence of Republican paramilitaries, you should be able to explain the key developments within loyalist paramilitarism.

## Faulkner replaces Chichester Clark

Levels of violence and destruction shot up during late 1970–early 1971 and Stormont demanded a stronger response from the new Conservative government. However, little happened – London didn't want to alienate nationalists. Chichester Clark therefore resigned on 20 March, to be replaced by Brian Faulkner.

# Internment

Faulkner was unable to reduce the levels of violence and, facing pressure for firm action, he reintroduced internment on 9 August 1971.

## Reasons for and effects of internment

Internment failed spectacularly:
- not one of the 452 men arrested was a leading member of PIRA
- despite the high levels of loyalist violence, the first loyalists were not interned until February 1973.

There were a number of responses to internment:
- At first unionists were happy; internment had worked before and they saw it as essential in ending PIRA violence. However, their support decreased when it failed to reduce violence.
- Nationalists saw internment as one-sided in its application. As a result PIRA membership increased.

Increased violence and destruction left many dead and thousands homeless. From then until the end of the year, 143 people died. Increasing Republican violence resulted in the establishment of the paramilitary UDA in September 1971.

Along with other nationalist and republican Labour representatives, the **SDLP** called for people to withhold payment of rents and rates and for a withdrawal from local government. Civil rights marches were also organised, but the Army's response also seemed to be hardening. A protest held at Magilligan Internment Camp on 22 January was met with baton charges and CS gas.

## Bloody Sunday, 1972, and responses to it

Following another anti-internment march in Derry/Londonderry eight days later, a riot developed. In response, troops from the Parachute Regiment shot thirteen men dead. Thirteen more were injured, one of whom later died of his wounds. Lord Widgery's official inquiry failed to provide a satisfactory explanation of the events of what became known as Bloody Sunday, although it did establish that none of those who died had been carrying a weapon when shot.

Bloody Sunday had a number of results:

**Table 4.2 Results of Bloody Sunday**

| Nationalist response | Unionist response |
|---|---|
| • Increased nationalist hostility to the state, symbolised by the burning of the British Embassy in Dublin.<br>• A growth in PIRA membership – particularly in Derry/Londonderry – and an increase in its bombing campaign. | • Continued support for the government which, while regretting the deaths, saw the march as illegal and provocative.<br>• The formation in February 1972 of Ulster Vanguard, headed by William Craig, the former Stormont minister. One of its meetings attracted 70,000 people. |

In addition, Britain faced international condemnation for its role in Northern Ireland.

> **What you need to know**
>
> You must be able to explain why internment was introduced, why it backfired and how it then linked in with the events that culminated in Bloody Sunday.

Option 2 Changing Relations: Northern Ireland and its Neighbours 1965–98

# Direct Rule

REVISED

## Reasons for the fall of Stormont

Faulkner now demanded the re-arming of the RUC and re-establishment of the B Specials. Westminster instead demanded control of law and order and justice; Faulkner refused. On 22 March Westminster revealed its plans to:

- transfer security control to Westminster
- hold a **referendum** on the future of the border
- gradually remove internment
- appoint a **Secretary of State** for Northern Ireland
- hold talks with other local parties in an attempt to establish a 'community government'.

> **What you need to know**
>
> You must be able to explain what **Direct Rule** was, identify why it was introduced and explain how the different sides responded to it.

## The introduction of direct rule

Unable to accept these proposals, the Stormont government resigned. Conservative Prime Minister Edward Heath responded by suspending Stormont for a year (later extended) and introducing Direct Rule. William Whitelaw was appointed as the first Secretary of State.

**Table 4.3 Reaction in Northern Ireland and in the Republic of Ireland**

| Unionist reaction | Nationalist reaction |
|---|---|
| • Most unionists were horrified at Stormont's end.<br>• Vanguard organised a series of massive protest strikes and shutdowns.<br>• There was also increased support for loyalist paramilitaries and a spate of sectarian killings, particularly in Belfast.<br>• Support for the DUP and other strongly unionist parties also increased. | • The SDLP and the Dublin government welcomed the chances for a new beginning.<br>• The IRA, although it had achieved one of its aims, stated its opposition to Direct Rule and announced its determination to continue its struggle to achieve a united Ireland.<br>• NICRA stated that its campaign would continue. |

## Revision task

TESTED

1 Write notes on:
- the reasons for the split in the IRA
- the differences between the OIRA and PIRA (post-split).

2 Explain how and why nationalist attitudes to the British Army changed in this period.

3 Write brief notes on the key developments/changes within unionist/loyalist politics in this period.

4 Analyse internment using the following headings:
- Reasons for its introduction
- Details
- Reasons for failure
- Responses/impact

5 Examine the events of Bloody Sunday under the following headings:
- Background
- Details
- British government reaction
- Other reactions

6 Draw up a table to explain the background to Direct Rule using the following headings:
- Faulkner's demands and Heath's response
- Heath's demands and Faulkner's response
- Heath's proposed changes and Stormont's response

7 Create a spider diagram indicating the different reactions to the suspension of Stormont/introduction of Direct Rule.

Exam practice answers at **www.hoddereducation.co.uk/myrevisionnotesdownloads**

## Exam practice

**2** Study Source B below and answer the question which follows:

### Source B

It is with great reluctance that the leadership of the IRA announces that the complete cessation of military operations will end at 6 p.m. on February 9. As we stated on August 31, 1994, the basis for the cessation was to enhance the democratic peace process and to underline our definitive [complete] commitment to its success.

We also made it clear that we believed that an opportunity to create a just and lasting settlement had been created.

The cessation presented an historic challenge for everyone and the IRA commends [praises] the leaderships of nationalist Ireland at home and abroad. They rose to the challenge. The British Prime Minister did not.

Instead of embracing the peace process, the British government acted in bad faith with Mr Major and the unionist leaders squandering this unprecedented [wasting this unexpected chance] opportunity to resolve the conflict.

Time and again, over the last 18 months, selfish party political and sectional [group] interests in the London parliament have been placed before the rights of the people of Ireland.

We take this opportunity to re-iterate [repeat] our total commitment to our republican objectives.

The resolution of the conflict in our country demands justice. It demands an inclusive negotiated settlement. That is not possible unless and until the British government faces up to its responsibilities.

The blame for the failure thus far of the Irish peace process lies squarely with John Major and his government.

> Provisional Irish Republican Army (PIRA) statement
> ending the ceasefire, 9 February 1996.

Give two reasons from Source B that explain why PIRA decided to end its ceasefire in February 1996. **[4]**

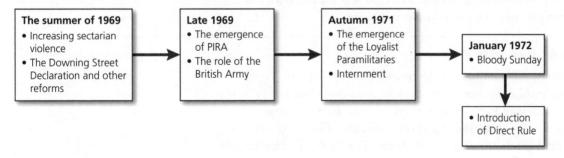

**The summer of 1969**
- Increasing sectarian violence
- The Downing Street Declaration and other reforms

**Late 1969**
- The emergence of PIRA
- The role of the British Army

**Autumn 1971**
- The emergence of the Loyalist Paramilitaries
- Internment

**January 1972**
- Bloody Sunday

- Introduction of Direct Rule

**Summary diagram:** A deteriorating situation, 1969–72

# 4 The search for a political solution – attempt at power-sharing, 1973–74

1972 was the worst year of the 'Troubles'. By the end of the year, 496 people had lost their lives in a series of atrocities which included:

- 21 July – Bloody Friday – when the PIRA detonated 20 bombs around Belfast, killing nine civilians
- 31 July when three PIRA bombs killed nine civilians in the village of Claudy in Co. Derry/Londonderry.

London responded on 31 July with **Operation Motorman**. This aimed to reclaim control of the paramilitary-controlled **no-go areas** established in Belfast, Derry/Londonderry and elsewhere in 1969.

## The reasons for and responses to the introduction of a power-sharing executive

REVISED

1973 began with increased levels of violence. Constant loyalist violence led to their internment in early February.

On 20 March 1973, London published its plans for the future of Northern Ireland. These proposed an assembly elected by proportional representation. There would also be an executive. However, it would not have control over security or justice. In addition, London insisted that there would have to be:

- the sharing of power between Catholics and Protestants
- the recognition of an 'Irish Dimension' through the creation of a Council of Ireland.

> **What you need to know**
>
> You must be able to explain what power-sharing was and how reactions to it undermined its chances of success. Equally important is your ability to explain what was agreed at Sunningdale and why this agreement was fatally flawed.

### Early problems

While nationalists were broadly supportive, unionists were divided in their reaction. Some of the OUP remained loyal to Brian Faulkner who supported the plans. Others – the remainder of the OUP, the DUP and the new Vanguard unionist Progressive Party (set up by William Craig) – formed the United Ulster Unionist Council (UUUC) to oppose the plans.

The results of the Assembly elections – held in June – revealed that the number of anti-power-sharing unionists elected was greater than the number of unionists who supported power-sharing.

### A Council of Ireland

On 21 November, the members of the power-sharing executive were announced. Six ministries were to be held by unionists, four by the SDLP and one by the Alliance Party. There would also be four non-voting members: two SDLP, one unionist and one Alliance. The OUP's Brian Faulkner would head the Executive, while the SDLP's Gerry Fitt would be his deputy.

The discussions about the Council of Ireland took place at Sunningdale in Berkshire. The meeting brought together the leading politicians from Britain, Ireland and Northern Ireland. At one stage Reverend Ian Paisley and William Craig were asked to attend to give their views. They refused.

## Terms of the Sunningdale Agreement

Agreement between the parties was finally reached in December 1973.

- London agreed not to oppose Irish unification if a majority of the Northern Ireland population desired it.
- Dublin accepted that Irish unity could only ever be achieved peacefully and with the consent of the majority of the people of Northern Ireland.
- A Council of Ministers with 14 members was to be established to help develop North–South co-operation. It would eventually be given decision-making powers.
- A 60-member Consultative Assembly would be elected by the *Dáil* and the Assembly.
- At some future date, control over internal security would be returned to the Assembly.
- Approval of the decisions made at Sunningdale was to take place at a future conference.

## Problems for the future

The problem was that both sides believed that they had agreed to something entirely different.

- The SDLP saw the agreement as leading to closer ties between Northern Ireland and the Republic of Ireland.
- Faulkner assented to the agreement to get Dublin to accept that Northern Ireland was part of the UK.

Republicans were also lukewarm, seeing the new system as proposing much less than what they sought.

Faulkner, however, now faced more serious problems. On 10 December, loyalist paramilitaries announced the formation of an Ulster **Army Council** to resist the 'Irish Dimension'. Nor did the PIRA seem any more satisfied, setting off a series of bombs in London.

The power-sharing executive took up office on 1 January 1974. Almost immediately its future was plunged into doubt by events within the OUP as a meeting of its ruling body, the Ulster Unionist Council, on 4 January, voted to reject Sunningdale. Faulkner immediately resigned as party leader to be replaced by Harry West. However, as Faulkner retained the support of most OUP Assembly members, he was able to remain at the head of the Executive.

## The general election of 1974

On 28 February a Westminster general election took place. Eleven of the twelve Northern Ireland constituencies were won by the UUUC. The only exception was Gerry Fitt, who retained his West Belfast seat for the SDLP. The election also resulted in a change in government in London, with Labour returning to power, under Harold Wilson.

## The UWC strike and its effects

On 14 May 1974 a general strike began, organised by the Ulster Workers' Council (UWC), a group of Protestant trade unionists who had gained substantial amounts of political and paramilitary support. Initially support was limited, but UDA intimidation and improved co-ordination by the UWC ensured that by the end of the week much of Northern Ireland had come to a standstill.

Tensions were further heightened on 17 May when car bombs exploded in Dublin and Monaghan. It was believed that loyalists were behind the attacks which claimed 27 lives (five more of the injured later died).

### Revision tasks

1. Analyse Britain's 1973 proposals for running Northern Ireland by writing a sentence about each of the following:
   - key elements of the proposals
   - Nationalist response
   - Unionist response
   - election results
   - Executive membership.
2. Create a spider diagram showing the key elements of the Sunningdale Agreement.
3. Analyse Sunningdale using the following headings:
   - Unionist understanding
   - Nationalist understanding
   - Republican reaction
   - Loyalist reaction

TESTED ☐

REVISED ☐

### What you need to know

The UWC strike destroyed the power-sharing experiment. Make sure that you can explain this development fully.

Although there were by now 17,500 soldiers in Northern Ireland, the Army was hesitant about taking on the strikers, arguing that the strike was a political action. Losing patience, Wilson appeared on television on 25 May to denounce the strike and call its organisers 'spongers'. His speech infuriated unionists and ensured that the strike continued.

## The re-introduction of Direct Rule

When the government ordered the Army to take over fuel supplies, the UWC ordered a total shutdown. Seeing no solution, Faulkner and the other unionist executive members resigned on 28 May, thus ending power-sharing.

Having achieved its goal, the UWC ended the strike on 29 May. The Assembly was suspended on 30 May and Direct Rule was re-introduced.

For the rest of the 1970s and into the 1980s, the British government continued with attempts to solve the Northern Ireland problem. At the same time, although the levels of violence lessened due to improved security measures, the PIRA launched a campaign of violence in Britain, exploding bombs in towns and cities such as Guildford and Birmingham.

**Revision tasks**

Analyse the UWC strike using the following headings:
- Reasons for the strike
- Levels of support
- Impact of strike
- Bombs in the Republic
- Wilson's speech
- Army involvement
- End of the strike

TESTED

## Exam practice

3 Study Source C and answer the question which follows:

### Source C

After a widespread consultative process ... and after having received confirmation and guarantees in relation to Northern Ireland's constitutional position within the United Kingdom, as well as other assurances, and, in the belief that the democratically expressed wishes of the greater number of people in Northern Ireland will be respected and upheld, the CLMC will universally cease all operational hostilities as from 12 midnight on Thursday 13th October 1994.

> Combined Loyalist Military Command (CLMC)
> Ceasefire Statement, 13 October 1994.

How useful is Source C for a historian studying the peace process of the 1990s?

Explain your answer, using Source C and your contextual knowledge. [5]

4 Study Source C again and answer the question below:

How reliable is Source C for a historian studying the peace process of the 1990s?

Explain your answer, using Source C and your contextual knowledge. [6]

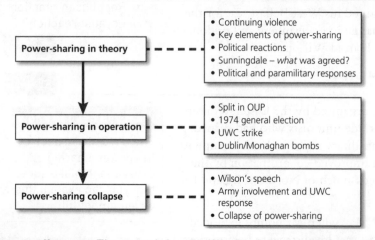

**Summary diagram:** The search for a political solution – attempt at power-sharing, 1973–4

# 5 Changing Republican strategy

## The reasons for the hunger strikes: new security policies

Following the collapse of power-sharing, the British government pursued policies of:

- **Ulsterisation** – reducing the strength of the Army, while increasing the size of the RUC and Ulster Defence Regiment (UDR)
- **criminalisation** – the end of special category status for those convicted of terrorist offences. This meant that those convicted after March 1976 would be treated in the same way as other criminals. They would be housed in a new prison consisting of H-shaped blocks, which had been built at the Maze outside Belfast.

PIRA prisoners – who saw themselves as soldiers fighting for Ireland's freedom – detested criminalisation. They protested with:

- a blanket protest: refusing to wear prison clothes and only covering themselves with a blanket
- a dirty protest: smearing their cell walls with excrement.

Later, when these protests received little support, prisoners attacked wardens and finally, in late 1980, PIRA prisoners began a hunger strike. This was called off in December as the prisoners (mistakenly) believed a deal had been reached on the wearing of their own clothes.

On 1 March 1981 a second hunger strike began, led by Bobby Sands, the PIRA prisoners' Commanding Officer. This time prisoners joined the protest at intervals, making the strike last longer and maximising its impact.

While the hunger strike gained huge publicity, it did not change government policy. Therefore, when the MP for Fermanagh–South Tyrone died, Republicans put Sands up as a candidate. On the fortieth day of his strike, Sands was elected to Westminster.

## The impact of the hunger strikes

Despite international pressure, neither side would compromise and on 5 May Sands died. The strike continued until 3 October 1981, by which time nine other prisoners had died. In the same period, 61 people lost their lives as a result of the violence that erupted in reaction to the hunger strikers' deaths.

> **What you need to know**
>
> The removal of **special category status** and the PIRA's reactions – particularly the hunger strike strategy – are key issues; can you explain all aspects of these developments?

## Concessions granted

No concessions were made during the hunger strike. However, within a week of its end a number were announced:

● prisoners could wear their own clothes
● the 50 per cent reduction in length of sentence lost by those involved in protests would be restored
● a greater number of prison visits would be permitted
● a greater degree of association among prisoners would be permitted.

These concessions resulted in the protests in favour of special category status all but ending by late October 1981.

In the aftermath of the hunger strikes, new problems were emerging for the British government:

● Increased nationalist alienation from the state, resulting from what was seen as Prime Minister Margaret Thatcher's approach to the hunger strikers, whose demands were viewed as reasonable.
● The growth in support for Republicanism.
● Unionists' increasing anxiety at the growth in PIRA support and the seeming weaknesses of security provisions which allowed PIRA violence to continue.
● The Irish government was pushing for the introduction of a new political initiative to end the Troubles.

Sands' election showed that there was much to gain from the political process. Therefore, at the 1981 **Ard Fheis**, delegates approved the movement's plan of contesting elections while also continuing to use violence to achieve its aims. This became known as the 'Armalite and Ballot Box' strategy.

## The effect of *Sinn Féin's* electoral success on the SDLP

The results of subsequent elections clearly revealed the growth in support for *Sinn Féin*. The party was soon winning local council seats. Then, in June 1983, party President, Gerry Adams won the West Belfast Westminster seat.

The British government was growing increasingly concerned that *Sinn Féin* might even replace the SDLP as the main nationalist party in the province. This prospect also worried the SDLP.

Revision tasks

1 Write definitions of:
● Ulsterisation
● criminalisation
● special category status.
2 Explain:
● the blanket and dirty protests
● the 1980 hunger strike.
3 Examine the 1981 hunger strike using the following headings:
● Key information about Bobby Sands
● Key dates and statistics
4 Create a spider diagram showing the concessions made after the strike ended.
5 Write brief notes on the emergence of the 'Armalite and Ballot Box' strategy – and its impact.

TESTED ☐

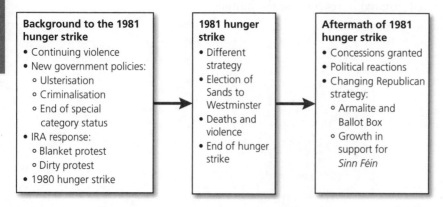

**Summary diagram:** Changing Republican strategy

# 6 Changing relations – towards closer co-operation

Faced with continuing violence and increasing support for *Sinn Féin*, the British and Irish governments decided to work more closely together. The outcome was the Anglo-Irish Agreement.

## Closer co-operation: the Anglo-Irish Agreement

REVISED

The agreement was signed on 15 November 1985 as:

- Thatcher realised that unless she dealt with nationalist alienation in Northern Ireland the security situation would not improve
- FitzGerald hoped that reduced nationalist alienation and reform of the security forces would undermine the minority's toleration of the PIRA and support for *Sinn Féin*.

**What you need to know**

There are three important areas for you to understand here: why the agreement was signed, what it said and how different groups and individuals reacted to it.

**Table 4.4 The four key terms**

| Key term 1 | Key term 2 | Key term 3 | Key term 4 |
|---|---|---|---|
| The establishment of an intergovernmental conference, headed by the Secretary of State and the Irish Foreign Minister.<br><br>This would deal with security, legal and political issues and improving cross-border co-operation. | A permanent **secretariat** made up of northern and southern civil servants. This would provide administrative support to the conference. | Devolution would only occur if there was agreement on power-sharing. | The agreement recognised that the Republic had a role to play in running Northern Ireland.<br><br>Dublin accepted that a united Ireland would only happen with the agreement of a majority within Northern Ireland. |

## The significance of the agreement

The agreement passed through both Westminster and the *Dáil* easily; however, it met with a wide variety of reactions elsewhere.

**Table 4.5 Reactions to the agreement**

| | Reaction |
|---|---|
| Unionists | Felt abandoned by their own government and believed that they were now in a process that would eventually result in a united Ireland. Annoyed that they had been kept in the dark during the negotiations. Only the Alliance Party did not condemn the agreement outright. |
| SDLP | Had more of a role in the creation of the agreement than any other party in Northern Ireland. Saw the accord as an opportunity to create a better way of life for all in the province. |
| *Sinn Féin* | Condemned the agreement, arguing that it made the division of Ireland more permanent since Dublin was now recognising the existence of Northern Ireland. |
| *Fianna Fáil* | The main opposition party – condemned the agreement due to the recognition being given by Dublin to Britain's right to be in Northern Ireland. |
| Individual politicians | Prominent Irish Labour Party Senator, Mary Robinson, resigned from her party because the agreement was unacceptable to the unionist community.<br><br>Ian Gow, a British Minister, resigned from the government arguing that the agreement was won by violence and would make the situation in the province worse rather than better. |

## The campaign against the agreement

Unionist politicians decided that the best way of opposing the Anglo-Irish Agreement was by a campaign of non-cooperation with the British government. They also wanted to show the depth of unionist opposition to what they termed the 'Dublin Diktat'.

The campaign against the agreement took a variety of forms:

● Marches to the headquarters of the new Anglo-Irish Secretariat. Sometimes these ended in violence.

● A huge protest rally at Belfast's City Hall on 23 November 1985 was attended by about 100,000 people.

● All 15 unionist MPs resigned their Westminster seats but then stood for re-election. They aimed to show the strength of unionist opposition through the total number of votes candidates received.

● A unionist 'Day of Action', held on 3 March 1986. Although much of the province was brought to a standstill using peaceful protest, in a number of places the protests resulted in violence.

● A campaign of civil disobedience with measures including the shunning of British ministers, the refusal to set rates in unionist-controlled councils and a **boycott** of Westminster.

● A loyalist campaign of violence and intimidation against the RUC. Then, in November 1986, Ulster Resistance, a paramilitary organisation that wanted to destroy the agreement, was formed.

## Results of the campaign

By and large, however, these tactics failed. The unionists gained a total of over 420,000 votes in the January 1986 **by-elections**; however, they lost a seat to the SDLP. The absence of 14 unionist MPs was not noticed at Westminster and since local councils had little power, their refusal to use this power made little or no difference. By September 1987, when the unionist leaders agreed to talk to British ministers again, it was clear that the campaign to destroy the agreement had failed.

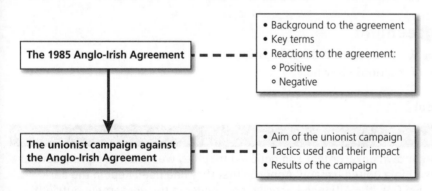

**Summary diagram:** Changing relations – towards closer co-operation

### Revision tasks

1 Analyse the Anglo-Irish Agreement using the following headings:
   ● Different reasons for signing
   ● Key terms
   ● Structures set up
   ● Main reactions
2 Create a spider diagram showing the different ways in which the unionist community showed its opposition to the agreement.
3 Taking each method of opposition in turn, indicate why it was a success or a failure.

TESTED

# 7 The Downing Street Declaration, 1993

## The Hume–Adams initiative

REVISED

In early 1988, SDLP leader John Hume began secret talks with *Sinn Féin* President, Gerry Adams. Hume believed that much could be gained from talking to Republicans, something no other party or government was prepared to do.

The Hume–Adams talks lasted eight months. They remained secret until April 1993, when they were revealed by a newspaper. By that time both politicians had started meeting again. The talks and Hume were severely criticised by other parties – and from within the SDLP.

In 1992, *Sinn Féin* published *Towards a Lasting Peace*. It focused on **self-determination** rather than armed struggle. It argued Britain should persuade unionists to join a united Ireland. It also argued that all nationalists should join together to achieve change. This would reduce the unionist majority within Northern Ireland to a minority within the whole island. When Britain saw that it could not continue to prop up unionism, it would deal with Republicans.

That this wasn't just wishful thinking had been proven by the Secretary of State, Peter Brooke:

- In 1989, he suggested that if the PIRA called a ceasefire, Westminster would respond imaginatively.
- He stated in November 1990 that Britain had no 'selfish strategic or economic interest' in remaining in Northern Ireland.
- He also approved the establishment of the 'Back Channel', a private line of communication with Republicans.

Brooke also attempted to kick-start discussions between the main constitutional parties regarding a political settlement. The main stumbling block for unionists was the Anglo-Irish Agreement. Therefore, to allow progress, the Intergovernmental Conference element of the 1985 Agreement was temporarily suspended.

## Progress?

Some progress was made. It was agreed that any settlement would have to involve three elements or 'strands':

- intercommunity relations
- North–South co-operation
- intergovernmental negotiations.

Final agreement would only come when consensus was reached in each of these areas. However, by mid-1991 talks had ended, collapsing over the timetable for each strand and over who would chair the North-South talks.

By mid-1992, the British general election had taken place and Sir Patrick Mayhew had become Secretary of State. That election also saw a reduction in *Sinn Féin's* share of the vote and the loss of Adams' seat in West Belfast to the SDLP. Mayhew also started talks based on the three-stranded framework. However, these ended within a few months.

> ### What you need to know
>
> The Hume–Adams talks mark the beginning of a new phase of the process that eventually resulted in the Good Friday Agreement. Make sure that you are able to explain just what was happening between 1988 and 1992.

# The Downing Street Declaration

REVISED

## The key terms and responses

Discussions between Hume and Adams recommenced in April 1993. They led to a *Sinn Féin* agreement to acknowledge the need for unionist consent with regard to the future of Northern Ireland.

The British and Irish governments could not accept this change as a basis for peace. Instead, in December 1993 they produced the Downing Street Declaration, which outlined their approach to peace. In the Declaration:

- Westminster undertook to 'uphold the democratic wish of a greater number of the people of Northern Ireland on the issue of whether they wish to support the Union or establish a sovereign united Ireland.' At the same time they restated that they had no 'selfish strategic or economic interest in Northern Ireland.'
- Dublin accepted that a united Ireland had to be the result of majority consent within Northern Ireland. It also accepted that parts of the 1937 Constitution were unacceptable to unionists and agreed – in the context of an overall settlement – to make changes to that document.

The British government also stated that they would not persuade unionists to join a united Ireland. They also reaffirmed that they still held **sovereignty** over Northern Ireland and did not contemplate sharing this with Dublin.

The Declaration led to different responses:

- *Sinn Féin* argued that the Declaration still allowed unionists a veto over its exercise.
- The Ulster Unionist Party (UUP), while liking parts of the Declaration, was less happy with its 'green tinge'.
- The DUP claimed that the Declaration was yet another step towards a united Ireland.
- Unionists were unpersuaded by the Declaration. In particular, they were concerned at the vague nature of the Republic's pledges to change its constitution. They argued that if the Republic was satisfied by any agreement, this would indicate its constitutional claim over Northern Ireland had been achieved.

> **What you need to know**
>
> The Downing Street Declaration is quite difficult to understand. Try to identify what the British and Irish governments were agreeing to – and make sure that you can explain how their ideas were responded to by nationalists and unionists.

> **Revision tasks**
>
> 1 Write brief notes on:
>    - The Hume–Adams talks
>    - *Towards a Lasting Peace*
>    - British government actions
>    - The 1992 general election
> 2 Create a table on the Downing Street Declaration using the headings:
>    - Terms
>    - Reactions
>
> TESTED

# The PIRA ceasefire

REVISED

Careful explanation of the Declaration – provided by Irish government representatives – enabled the PIRA to announce the 'complete cessation of military operations' as of 31 August 1994. The statement recognised the 'potential of the current situation' but warned that *Sinn Féin* would have to be included in any talks process.

Initial reactions to the statement were positive:

- *Taoiseach* Albert Reynolds shook hands with Gerry Adams. A month later, Dublin announced the establishment of a Forum for Peace and Reconciliation, to be attended by representatives of all Irish parties.
- In early December, nine PIRA inmates were released **on licence**.
- President Bill Clinton allowed Adams into the USA and organised conferences aimed at supporting the peace process with economic investment.

However, London stated that it wanted to hear the word 'permanent' in connection with the PIRA cessation and added that it needed time to test the PIRA's actions rather than its words.

> **What you need to know**
>
> The 1994 ceasefires were historic developments. Examiners will want you to be able to explain how they came about, what they stated and just what happened in their aftermath.

Within four months, however, the Dublin part of this support network had crumbled. In December 1994, Reynolds' *Fianna Fáil* administration was replaced by a *Fine Gael*–Labour–Democratic Left coalition. The new *Taoiseach*, John Bruton, was not known for his love of Republicanism.

Loyalist paramilitaries waited a further six weeks before announcing their ceasefire (13 October 1994). By the end of 1994, their political representatives – the Progressive Unionist Party (PUP) and the Ulster Democratic Party (UDP) – were engaged in discussions with representatives of the London government.

## The Framework Documents

In February 1995, the London and Dublin governments published the Framework Documents.

The first paper, *A Framework for Accountable Government in Northern Ireland*, outlined Britain's proposals for new political institutions for Northern Ireland. These included:
● a 90-strong assembly that would exercise powers similar to its 1974 power-sharing predecessor
● a range of protections for the nationalist minority.

The second document, *A New Framework for Agreement*, was produced jointly by London and Dublin. It was based around the principles of self-determination, consent, non-violence and **parity of esteem**. To help develop relationships within Ireland, it proposed:
● the establishment of some form of North–South body
● that relations between Britain and Ireland would be underpinned by structures similar to those established by the Anglo-Irish Agreement.

Reactions from local parties were mixed:
● Unionists saw too many similarities with Sunningdale and hated the possibility of the development of North–South links into some form of institutions with executive powers.
● *Sinn Féin* argued that the Framework Documents provided mechanisms by which unionists would be able to veto progress.
● Only the SDLP and Alliance reacted positively.

## The collapse of the ceasefire

The lack of face-to-face talks between the British government and Republicans began to impact on the peace process. The main problem was **decommissioning**, which for the PIRA meant defeat and surrender. Its frustration boiled over and so it began to plan for a return to military operations.

Unaware of this, London established the Mitchell Commission (chaired by former US Senate Majority Leader George Mitchell) to look into decommissioning, which reported its findings in early 1996. It suggested the handover of weapons in parallel with talks taking place, but not before. It also proposed principles of non-violence, which all parties would have to sign up to.

## Obstacles to peace

Mitchell's work should have provided a way forward, but there were yet more obstacles to overcome:
● The decision to hold elections to a Peace Forum – an idea first raised by the Mitchell Commission – as a way of providing a mandate for the participants.

## Revision tasks

1 Create a timeline of key developments between August and December 1994.
2 Create a table on the Framework Documents using the headings:
   ● Terms of Document One
   ● Terms of Document Two
   ● Reactions
3 Write brief notes on:
   ● PIRA problems
   ● The Mitchell Commission

TESTED ☐

REVISED ☐

- The collapse of the PIRA cessation in February 1996. This was proof enough for all of the doubters that the Republican movement had never seen its cessation as anything more than a tactic.

The PIRA blamed the British government's reluctance to move the peace process forward for its decision to return to violence. It has been suggested that one of the main reasons for this was the position that the Conservative government found itself in by that time. Prime Minister John Major – who relied on the support of unionist MPs to stay in power – could only push the process forward at a pace with which the unionists were comfortable.

Unionists supported the Forum plan but nationalists were furious. In their view, the plan was yet another stalling exercise, an example of the influence that the unionist parties in general and the UUP in particular had over the British government.

In spite of their hostility to the plan, both the SDLP and *Sinn Féin* put forward candidates for the Forum elections. However, *Sinn Féin* announced that it would boycott the resulting assembly, while the SDLP announced that it would decide to attend the Forum on a day-by-day basis, depending on what the agenda was.

## Election results

- Support for the DUP and *Sinn Féin* had increased.
- The UDP and PUP won seats, which meant that they would be able to attend any future peace talks. This enabled negotiations that might bring all the key players in the process along.

The peace talks finally began in June 1996. However, the absence of a PIRA ceasefire meant that *Sinn Féin* was not present. Indeed, the entire process was in some form of limbo throughout 1996 and during the first half of 1997. It appeared that no real progress would be possible until a stronger government had been installed in London.

### What you need to know

The road to peace proved to be difficult. You need to be able to explain what happened at each stage, what difficulties emerged – and how these were overcome.

### Revision task

Write brief notes on:
- The collapse of the PIRA ceasefire
- The Peace Forum
  - Aims
  - Reactions
- Election

TESTED

**Summary diagram:** The Downing Street Declaration, 1993

# 8 The Good Friday Agreement, 1998

Following the May 1997 Westminster general election:

- Tony Blair, the new Labour Prime Minister, announced that if the PIRA renewed its ceasefire, *Sinn Féin* would be allowed to enter talks.
- Support for the Republican movement grew – *Sinn Féin* were successful: Martin McGuinness won a seat in Mid Ulster, and Gerry Adams regained the West Belfast seat that he had lost in 1992.

At the same time an election in the Republic of Ireland (June 1997) saw Bertie Ahern become *Taoiseach*.

## The creation of the Good Friday Agreement

REVISED

Having been assured that it would be included in talks, the PIRA ceasefire was renewed on 20 July 1997. Then, having signed up to the Mitchell Principles of Non-Violence, *Sinn Féin* entered the talks in September 1997.

At that point the DUP and the UKUP walked out and refused to even consider **proximity negotiations**. The UUP and the parties representing the loyalist paramilitaries remained in the process.

It was important that *Sinn Féin* could negotiate without the PIRA beginning its campaign again. A **General Army Convention** was therefore called and agreed a change to the PIRA's constitution that would allow its Army Council to decide on possible concessions. This led a section of the Republican movement to leave and set up a new paramilitary grouping, the Real IRA.

It had already been decided that the negotiations would be based around three strands:

- Strand One would concentrate on establishing a suitable internal governmental structure for Northern Ireland.
- Strand Two would be concerned with relationships between the two parts of Ireland.
- Strand Three would deal with British–Irish relations.

At the same time, an Independent International Commission on Decommissioning was launched under the chairmanship of Canadian General John de Chastelain.

After missing the final deadline for the talks it seemed that UUP objections to decommissioning and the release of paramilitary prisoners might lead to the collapse of the process. US President Bill Clinton, however, used his powers of persuasion to keep negotiations going.

On Friday 10 April 1998, Good Friday, a deal was finally done.

> **What you need to know**
>
> Examiners will want you to be able to identify and write about the background to and main terms of the Good Friday Agreement.

**Table 4.6 The key terms of the Good Friday Agreement**

| Strand | Key terms |
|---|---|
| Strand One | Dealt with the internal political settlement. It established a 108-member Assembly, elected by proportional representation (PR). It would have full legislative and executive authority over areas previously administered by the Northern Ireland Office (the government department that ran Northern Ireland). |
| Strand Two | Focused on relations within the island of Ireland. It established a North–South Ministerial Council that would be responsible for cross-border co-operation in areas including language, agriculture, health, tourism and trade. Meetings of the Council would include the relevant ministers from both **jurisdictions** depending on the issues under discussion. |
| Strand Three | Centred on East–West relations, namely those between Ireland and Britain. There would be a Council of the Isles or British–Irish Council comprising members from all parliaments and devolved assemblies within the British Isles. It would enable consultation and co-operation in a range of areas including drugs, agriculture, energy and regional issues. There would also be a British–Irish Intergovernmental Conference similar to the institutions established by the 1985 Anglo-Irish Agreement. |

## Other elements of the Good Friday Agreement

There were other significant elements.
- The Irish government undertook to renounce its constitutional claims to Northern Ireland as contained within Articles II and III of the 1937 Irish Constitution.
- The British government agreed to replace the 1920 Government of Ireland Act.
- There were also to be prisoner releases, coupled with the decommissioning of paramilitary weapons.
- The Agreement also established an Independent Commission on Policing in Northern Ireland.

## The responses to the Good Friday Agreement

REVISED

It was clear that there were going to be difficulties in selling the Agreement, particularly within unionism.
- The DUP and the UKUP had walked out of the negotiations.
- Divisions were now emerging within the UUP. Six of the UUP's ten MPs opposed the deal.
- In May, all the unionists opposed to the Agreement set up the United Unionist Campaign to co-ordinate their campaign of opposition.

At first, the Republican response also provided cause for concern. On 30 April, the PIRA stated that the Agreement fell 'short of presenting a solid basis for a lasting settlement', and added that it would not decommission any weapons.

However, a few days later, *Sinn Féin* advised its supporters to back the Agreement. Then at the Party's *Ard Fheis*, its constitution was changed so as to allow members to take seats in the Northern Ireland Assembly.

> **What you need to know**
>
> How different groups responded to the Good Friday Agreement is obviously important. Make sure that you are able to write about these responses – and what they meant for the chances of a lasting peace.

Exam practice answers at **www.hoddereducation.co.uk/myrevisionnotesdownloads**

## The referendums

The first real test of the Good Friday Agreement were the referendums held on both sides of the border on 22 May 1998.

1 Within Northern Ireland, 71.12 per cent of those who voted supported the Agreement. The overall turnout was 80.98 per cent, a figure significantly higher than that produced at most election times.
2 Insofar as estimates can be relied upon, it seemed that close to 97 per cent of nationalists and 52 per cent of unionists supported the Agreement. This limited majority (within unionism), gave significant cause for concern in terms of the Agreement's chances of success.
3 The figures for the referendum in the Republic were even clearer. 94.4 per cent agreed with the plans to amend Articles II and III of the Irish Constitution.

## The new Assembly

Elections for the new Assembly were held in late June.

On the surface it seemed that there was a clear majority of members elected in favour of power-sharing (80 out of 108 Assembly members). However, this failed to take account of two important qualifications.
- Not all of the 28 UUP members elected were in favour of the Agreement.
- The Agreement said that certain decisions (called key decisions) needed majority support from both communities. Given unionist divisions, that was going to be hard to archieve.

The new Assembly met for the first time on 15 July 1998 with the Alliance Party's Lord John Alderdice having been appointed Presiding Officer by the Secretary of State. David Trimble, UUP Leader, and Seamus Mallon, SDLP Deputy-Leader, were elected as First and deputy First Ministers (Designate).

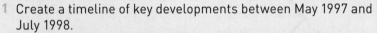

## Revision tasks

TESTED ☐

1 Create a timeline of key developments between May 1997 and July 1998.
2 Create a table showing the position of the different political parties on the peace process. Use the following headings:
   - Name
   - Position on
     - The negotiations leading up to the Good Friday Agreement
     - The terms of the Agreement
     - The post-Agreement referendums
3 Create a spider diagram illustrating the main terms of the Good Friday Agreement.

# Exam practice

**5 a** Name the British Prime Minister from 1997. [1]
**b** Give one reason for the introduction of the Anglo-Irish Agreement in 1985. [1]
**c** Give one term of the first Framework Document of 1995. [1]
**d** Describe one reason why there was nationalist opposition to the 1996 Peace Forum. [1]

**6** Explain two of the following:
**A** The reasons for O'Neill's downfall in 1969
**B** The different responses to Bloody Sunday in 1972
**C** The impact of the UWC Strike in 1974

Explanation One: (A, B or C)

Explanation Two: (B or C if you chose A;

A or B if you chose C; A or C if you chose B) [9 + 9]

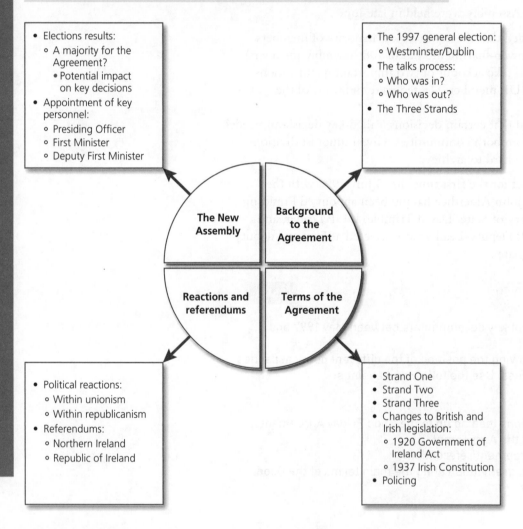

- Elections results:
  - A majority for the Agreement?
    - Potential impact on key decisions
  - Appointment of key personnel:
    - Presiding Officer
    - First Minister
    - Deputy First Minister

- The 1997 general election:
  - Westminster/Dublin
- The talks process:
  - Who was in?
  - Who was out?
- The Three Strands

**The New Assembly**

**Background to the Agreement**

**Reactions and referendums**

**Terms of the Agreement**

- Political reactions:
  - Within unionism
  - Within republicanism
- Referendums:
  - Northern Ireland
  - Republic of Ireland

- Strand One
- Strand Two
- Strand Three
- Changes to British and Irish legislation:
  - 1920 Government of Ireland Act
  - 1937 Irish Constitution
- Policing

**Summary diagram:** The Good Friday Agreement, 1998

# International Relations, 1945–2003

## 1 Co-operation ends and the Cold War begins

### The breakdown of the wartime alliance between the USA and USSR

REVISED

The Second World War (1939 to 1945) was fought between:

**The Allies**
- Britain
- The USA
- The Soviet Union (USSR)
- China
- France

**The Axis**
- Germany
- Italy
- Japan

By 1945, Germany and Japan had been defeated. The USA and USSR were now the world's main superpowers. Within months of the war, the USA and the USSR had become engaged in a new struggle that came to be called the Cold War.

### Ideological differences: the origins of the Cold War

REVISED

Post-war relations between the USA and the USSR broke down because of their ideological differences. These differences go back the Russian Revolution in October 1917 when the communist **Bolsheviks** took over Russia. They wanted to destroy **capitalist democracies** like the USA.

**Table 5.1 The main differences between capitalist and communist systems**

|  | Capitalist democracies | Communist countries |
| --- | --- | --- |
| Political system | Free choice in elections | No choice in elections |
| Media | Freedom of speech | No freedom of speech |
| Wealth | Individuals own their own property | The government owns all property |

Distrust grew in the years that followed.
- Britain, France, Japan and the USA helped the Bolsheviks' opponents in the Russian civil war (1917–22).
- Britain and the USA refused to recognise the communist government for years after the revolution.
- Britain and France refused to work with Russia against Nazi Germany.

**What you need to know**

You need to know which countries fought on which side during the Second World War.

**Revision task**

Draw a mind map to show which countries fought on which side in the Second World War.

TESTED

**What you need to know**

You need to be able to explain how the USA and USSR were able to work together during the Second World War despite having very different ideologies.

**Revision task**

Make notes on the main features of the following:
- capitalism
- communism.

TESTED

Stalin, the leader of the Soviet Union (USSR), as Russia was now called, began a series of Five-Year Plans to ensure that they would be ready to fight a war against the capitalist West. When Britain and France did not help him against Nazi Germany, Stalin signed a Non-Aggression Pact with Hitler in 1939. The USSR did not go to war against the Nazis when the Second World War began, because it was not ready to go to war.

### Fighting a common enemy (before 1945)

When Germany invaded the Soviet Union in June 1941, Stalin joined the Allies. The Soviets suffered heavy losses during the Nazi invasion, but Britain and the USA ignored Stalin's demands for an attack from the west to distract the Nazis until D-Day in 1944. Stalin believed that they hoped Germany and the USSR would destroy each other.

When the Soviets stopped the Nazis' advance, they began to drive them back into Germany. Churchill tried to persuade the Americans to stop this, but President Roosevelt (1933–45) trusted Stalin. The alliance held together until it was clear that the war was coming to an end.

## Yalta, February 1945

REVISED ☐

In February 1945, the Big Three (Churchill, Roosevelt and Stalin) met at Yalta in the Ukraine to decide what would happen in post-war Europe. Each leader had different aims.
- Churchill saw the USSR as a danger to the West that had to be stopped – it was gaining control of countries like Poland.
- Roosevelt wanted a free world protected by the **United Nations (UN)**. He hoped the USSR would join the UN.
- Stalin wanted friendly (communist) countries between Western Europe and the USSR to protect against further attack.

**What you need to know**

You need to be able to explain how decisions taken at the Yalta conference increased mistrust between the USA and USSR.

### Decisions made at Yalta

They managed to agree that:
- Germany and Berlin would be divided into four zones and be occupied by the Allies
- Germany would pay **reparations**
- the new UN would help keep the peace
- the USSR would declare war on Japan
- Poland would have new borders
- Eastern Europe would come under the influence of the USSR.

## Potsdam, July 1945

REVISED ☐

By the time they met again at Potsdam in July 1945, several changes had taken place:
- Hitler was dead – the war in Europe was over.
- US troops were preparing to return home.
- Soviet troops were stationed in Eastern Europe.
- Roosevelt had been replaced as President by Harry Truman (1945–53) who did not like Stalin.
- Clement Attlee replaced Churchill as Britain's Prime Minister.
- The Americans and British worried about the USSR stripping Germany of resources and putting communist governments in control of Eastern Europe.

**What you need to know**

You need to be able to explain how decisions at Potsdam forced the former Allies further apart.

## Decisions made at Potsdam

The meeting was less friendly than before. They agreed:

- how Germany and Austria were to be divided and occupied
- changes to Germany's border with Poland and Poland's border with the USSR.

There was a lot of disagreement about the future of Europe. The wartime alliance was breaking up. This was the first step towards the Cold War.

## Hiroshima and Nagasaki

REVISED

Meanwhile, the war in the Pacific against Japan continued. At Iwo Jima (February–March 1945) and Okinawa (April–June 1945), the Japanese fought hard. American generals feared the invasion of Japan itself might kill a million American soldiers.

President Truman feared that the USSR would try to establish **communism** in the Pacific as they had already done in Eastern Europe. At Potsdam, Truman did not directly tell Stalin that the USA had developed an atomic bomb, but he became more assertive towards the USSR.

### The Atomic Age

On 6 August 1945, the USA dropped an atomic bomb on the Japanese city of Hiroshima. A quarter of a million people were killed. Three days later, the Americans dropped another bomb on Nagasaki. The Japanese surrendered on 14 August.

Stalin was furious that his allies had not shared the atomic bomb with him. He thought it was used to intimidate the USSR. He accused the USA of using its atomic power to build an empire. This caused the final breakdown of US-Soviet relations.

### The start of the Cold War

Stalin's scientists built an atomic bomb by 1949. By the 1950s, both superpowers had enough weapons to destroy the world. The USA and the USSR were at war. However, they had to fight a 'cold war' to avoid nuclear destruction.

---

**What you need to know**

You need to explain how the use of **atomic bombs** to end the war with Japan increased tensions between the USA and USSR.

---

**Revision tasks**

1 For each of these events explain how they drove the USA and USSR further apart:
- the Yalta conference
- the Potsdam conference
- the atomic bomb.

2 Which event do you think was the most important in driving the USA and USSR apart after the Second World War? Explain your choice.

TESTED

---

| Ideological differences | | |
|---|---|---|
| **Yalta conference** (February 1945) <br> • Germany and Berlin to be divided <br> • Eastern Europe in the Soviet sphere of influence <br> • USSR to declare war on Japan <br> • UN would keep the peace after the war | **Potsdam conference** (July 1945) <br> • Less friendly <br> • Disagreements about reparations and communist governments in Eastern Europe <br> • Agreed changed borders Germany/Poland/USSR | **Hiroshima & Nagasaki** (August 1945) <br> • 6 August atomic bomb dropped on Hiroshima, 9 August on Nagasaki by USA <br> • Stalin furious he was not told about this new weapon <br> • USSR builds atomic bomb, 1949 |

**Summary digram:** Co-operation ends and the Cold War begins

# 2 Emerging superpower rivalry and its consequences, 1945–49

## The Soviet takeover of Eastern Europe

REVISED

By the end of 1945 the USA and USSR:
● were superpowers
● worried the other wanted to spread its ideology
● believed their opponent wanted to destroy them
● became suspicious and defensive towards each other.

### What you need to know

You need to be able to explain how the Soviet occupation of Eastern Europe drove the USA and USSR further apart.

### The actions of the USSR in Eastern Europe, 1945–49

By 1945, the Soviet Army had taken over most of the countries in Eastern Europe and stayed there. Stalin promised democratic elections. Between 1945 and 1947, these elections gave power to governments friendly to the USSR. There was a suspicion that the elections had been rigged, but the USSR denied it.

By 1947 these countries were ruled by communists:
● Albania – communists seized power in 1945, then held an election with only communist candidates
● Bulgaria – communists took power in a rigged election in 1946
● Hungary – communists, led by Mátyás Rákosi, gradually took over the running of the country
● Poland – 1947 elections resulted in a communist government after non-communist politicians had been sent to the USSR
● Romania – mass demonstrations forced a communist government into power in 1945.

The Soviets already controlled eastern Germany and communist Tito controlled Yugoslavia. Czechoslovakia became communist in 1948 after communists organised armed demonstrations and a general strike.

The USA thought the Soviets were building an empire in Eastern Europe. Stalin wanted to create a '**buffer zone**' to protect the USSR from a future invasion. He wanted these countries to be loyal to the Soviet Union. To take over countries, the USSR would:
● make sure communists got important positions in post-war governments
● suggest changes to help economic recovery and gain support for the communists
● control elections to ensure a communist victory
● control the population using secret police.

### The response of the USA and its allies

Each side was very suspicious of what the other side was doing.
● Truman adopted the policy of **containment** – the USA would act to stop the further spread of communism.
● The buffer zone increased America's fear of the USSR and containment increased the USSR's fear of the USA.

### Revision tasks

1 Describe and explain the USSR's 'buffer zone'.
2 Describe USA's policy of containment.
3 Explain the relationship between the buffer zone and containment under the following two headings:
   ● How did the buffer zone lead to containment?
   ● How did containment increase the need for a buffer zone?

TESTED

# The emergence of the Cold War and the impact on relations, 1946–47

REVISED

## Churchill's Iron Curtain speech

In a speech in Fulton, Missouri in March 1946, Churchill said Stalin had spread communism behind an 'iron curtain'. He argued that the USA and USSR should stop communism from spreading. This made Stalin angry – he believed he was just protecting his own country.

> **What you need to know**
>
> You need to be able to explain how events in 1946 and 1947 made tensions in the Cold War even worse.

## The Truman Doctrine and Marshall Plan

### Events in Greece

The Allies had agreed to help the Greek Army, which was fighting a civil war against Greek communists. In March 1947, the British government said it could no longer afford to fund this. Truman worried that if Greece became communist, communism could spread to the oil-rich Middle East.

### The Truman Doctrine

Truman told the US Congress that it would now be America's policy to use military or economic means to stop countries becoming communist through invasion or revolution. This was called the **Truman Doctrine**. Congress released $400 million to end the communist threat in Greece.

### The Marshall Plan

Truman believed that if America could help build up the economies of poorer countries, they would not become communist and could start trading with the USA. US Secretary of State, George Marshall, wanted to invest $13.3 billion into Europe, if countries agreed to open their markets to American goods. This was known as the Marshall Plan or Marshall Aid. The money was spent on defence and armaments, as well as roads, machinery and factories.

### Reactions to the Marshall Plan

Congress was not sure about the Marshall Plan. They changed their mind after the Communist takeover of Czechoslovakia in 1948.

Sixteen countries, including Britain and western Germany, benefited from the Plan, which was overseen by the Organisation for European Economic Co-operation (OEEC).

Stalin argued that the USA was trying to gain influence over countries by controlling their economies. He rejected the offer of money. He:
- established the Communist Information Bureau (Cominform) in 1947 to get communist countries working together
- set up the Council for Mutual Economic Assistance (Comecon) in 1949 to encourage economic co-operation behind the Iron Curtain.

# Impact of the Truman Doctrine and Marshall Plan

Both the Truman Doctrine and Marshall Plan mark a significant development in the Cold War. The Marshall Plan played a vital part in the economic reconstruction of Europe. However, it might also have made Cold War relations worse.

## Revision tasks

TESTED

1 Why did the 'iron curtain' speech make Stalin angry?
2 Explain how the Truman Doctrine and Marshall Plan contributed to the following:
   ● making capitalist countries safer
   ● making tensions with the USSR worse.

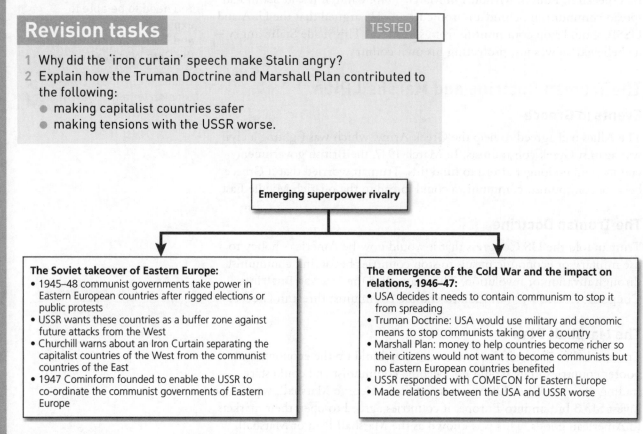

**Emerging superpower rivalry**

**The Soviet takeover of Eastern Europe:**
- 1945–48 communist governments take power in Eastern European countries after rigged elections or public protests
- USSR wants these countries as a buffer zone against future attacks from the West
- Churchill warns about an Iron Curtain separating the capitalist countries of the West from the communist countries of the East
- 1947 Cominform founded to enable the USSR to co-ordinate the communist governments of Eastern Europe

**The emergence of the Cold War and the impact on relations, 1946–47:**
- USA decides it needs to contain communism to stop it from spreading
- Truman Doctrine: USA would use military and economic means to stop communists taking over a country
- Marshall Plan: money to help countries become richer so their citizens would not want to become communists but no Eastern European countries benefited
- USSR responded with COMECON for Eastern Europe
- Made relations between the USA and USSR worse

**Summary diagram:** Emerging superpower rivalry and its consequences, 1945–49

# 3 Flashpoints in Europe and the impact on international relations

## The actions of the USSR in Eastern Europe

REVISED

There were four main confrontations between the superpowers in Europe.

**What you need to know**

You need to understand why the actions of the USSR in Eastern Europe increased tension with the USA during the Cold War.

## 1 The Berlin Blockade and Airlift, 1948–49

REVISED

After the Second World War, Germany was divided into four zones, each to be controlled by the British, Americans, Soviets and French. Berlin was also divided, but as it was in the Soviet zone.

**What you need to know**

You need to understand why the USSR blockaded Berlin in 1948 and how the USA tried to get round it.

### Causes of the Berlin Blockade and Airlift

#### Different aims

The USA and USSR had different ideas about what to do with Germany.
- The USSR wanted Germany weak so it could not invade other countries again.
- The USA wanted Germany to recover so it could help stop the spread of communism.

#### Different economies

By 1948 there was economic recovery in Western Germany because of Marshall Aid. Because the USSR had taken resources from the Soviet zone, life was much poorer there than in the western zones.

#### A new currency

The USA, Britain and France united their zones into 'Trizonia' in March 1948. They introduced a new currency, the Deutschmark, to help with economic recovery. Stalin thought it would disturb the Germans living in poverty under communist rule in East Berlin.

### The events of the Berlin Blockade

On 24 June 1948, Stalin closed all the roads, railways and canals connected to West Berlin. Stalin hoped that he could force the Western powers to leave Berlin as they would quickly run out of supplies. The USA had to hold on to Berlin as it symbolised their policy of challenging communist rule.

### The events of the Berlin Airlift

Truman decided to airlift supplies into West Berlin to break the blockade. If Stalin shot down a plane he risked starting another war. The USA flew in 13,000 tonnes of supplies every day. There was strict rationing in West Berlin. After a year Stalin admitted defeat and the blockade was lifted. Two million tonnes of supplies had been transported and 101 men had died, mostly in plane crashes.

**Revision tasks**

1 Explain the causes of the Berlin Blockade in 1948.
2 How successful was the Berlin Airlift in tackling the Berlin Blockade? Why was this?

TESTED

## The consequences and impact on relations

The airlift was a propaganda victory for the USA. Containment had worked.

In April 1949, 12 Western nations set up the **North Atlantic Treaty Organisation (NATO)** to help prevent a Soviet attack. An attack on one NATO member would be considered as an attack on them all.

In May 1949, the Federal Republic of Germany (known as West Germany) was established. In October the USSR renamed its zone the German Democratic Republic (East Germany).

The Soviets saw NATO as an aggressive alliance, especially when West Germany was allowed to join in 1955. The Warsaw Pact was established in May 1955 to be a communist version of NATO.

# 2 Hungary, 1956

REVISED

## Causes of the uprising

### Background to the uprising: 'The Thaw'

Stalin died in 1953. By 1955, Nikita Khrushchev had become leader of the USSR. He said he wanted a thaw in the Cold War. In 1955–56, Khrushchev:

- apologised for how Stalin had treated Yugoslavia
- met with leaders of the West in Geneva
- denounced Stalin's policies
- said he wanted '**peaceful co-existence**' with non-communist nations
- **de-Stalinised** the USSR
- ordered the breaking up of Cominform.

The USA hoped there would be more freedom in Eastern Europe and a higher standard of living for the people there.

Because this was slow to happen, there were riots and demonstrations in Poland and Czechoslovakia in July 1956. A full-scale rebellion happened in Hungary in October–November 1956.

> **What you need to know**
>
> You need to be able to explain why there was an uprising against the communist regime in Hungary and why it failed.

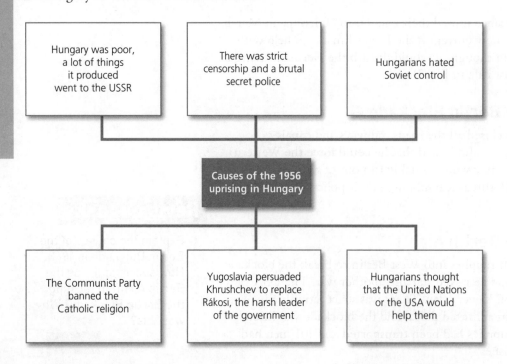

Hungary was poor, a lot of things it produced went to the USSR

There was strict censorship and a brutal secret police

Hungarians hated Soviet control

**Causes of the 1956 uprising in Hungary**

The Communist Party banned the Catholic religion

Yugoslavia persuaded Khrushchev to replace Rákosi, the harsh leader of the government

Hungarians thought that the United Nations or the USA would help them

Exam practice answers at **www.hoddereducation.co.uk/myrevisionnotesdownloads**

# The crushing of dissent

**Table 5.2** The events of the rebellion

| Date | Event |
|------|-------|
| 23 October | Hungarian students took to the streets to demand reform. |
| 26 October | Imre Nagy, a moderate communist, was made leader. |
| 1 November | Nagy said Hungary would have free elections and withdraw from the Warsaw Pact. |
| 4 November | 6,000 Soviet tanks were sent to put down the revolt. |

## The consequences and impact on relations

- The USSR's actions showed it would not let a member of the Warsaw Pact leave as it would leave the USSR open to attack, or lead to the breakup of the Pact.
- The West decided not to attack the USSR in Eastern Europe, but turned its attention to stopping the spread of communism in Asia instead.
- Khrushchev talked of peaceful co-existence, but he did not seem to want to change anything.

# 3 Berlin, 1959–61

## Reasons for growing tension

In Berlin it was possible for people to flee to the capitalist West. They wanted to leave to live a better quality of life in the West. Two million people, mostly skilled workers, escaped this way. The USSR was embarrassed about this.

Khrushchev was also worried that West Berlin was being used for spying on the communist East. He tried to force the West to leave in Paris in 1960 and Vienna in 1961 but he failed.

## The building of the Berlin Wall

By 1960 so many people were escaping to West Berlin it was causing labour shortages in the East. Khrushchev decided to end this situation. In August 1961 he ordered a massive wall to be built to divide the city permanently. Anyone trying to cross the wall ran the risk of being shot. The number of defections to the West reduced dramatically.

## The response of the West

America protested but did nothing. In private the USA was relieved. Berlin was a cause of tension which the Soviets had now closed down.

## The consequences and impact on relations

Anti-communist feeling in the West increased. The Berlin Wall became a symbol of the divisions between East and West. It became a symbol of what capitalists thought was wrong with communism.

**Revision tasks**

1 Explain the background to the uprising in Hungary.
2 How successful was the uprising in Hungary? Explain why.

TESTED

REVISED

**What you need to know**

You need to explain why the Berlin Wall was built and how it increased tensions in the Cold War.

**Revision task**

Make a list of the ways that events in Berlin made relations between the USA and USSR worse.

TESTED

# 4 Czechoslovakia, 1968

## Causes of the 'Prague Spring'

Khrushchev was replaced by Leonid Brezhnev in 1964. In January 1968, the moderate Alexander Dubček became leader of Czechoslovakia. There had been demonstrations, directed against the lack of civil rights and poor standard of living. Czechs resented that their industrial products were sent to the USSR while they were in poverty. Students resented restrictions on freedom. Writers wanted freedom of speech.

Dubček wanted Czechoslovakia to remain communist but knew reform was needed. He introduced an 'Action Programme' of political and economic reforms that included:

- freedom of speech
- more economic freedom
- increased foreign trade
- allowing travel abroad
- reducing the power of the secret police.

The reforms were popular. They became known as the 'Prague Spring'.

## The Soviet response

Brezhnev was afraid that these reforms would lead other countries to do the same. In July, the USSR and other communist countries wrote to Czechoslovakia to object. Dubček said Czechoslovakia would remain in the Warsaw Pact. Brezhnev ordered 400,000 troops into the country on 20 August 1968. He said Czech communists had invited them. It was officially a Warsaw Pact operation, but in reality was mostly Soviet.

Dubček told Czechs to show their opposition through peaceful resistance. There were some instances of violent resistance. Dubček was called to Moscow and subsequently said the 'Prague Spring' had ended. He resigned, to be replaced by the hard-line Gustav Husak.

The repression of the Prague Spring was not as violent as in Hungary. Eighty people were killed and Dubček was demoted not executed. Those who supported reform lost their jobs and homes and were put under constant observation.

There was hardly any violent resistance to the Soviet invasion, but some students burned themselves to death in protest.

## The response of the West and the impact on relations

The invasion did not damage relations very much, although communism became even less popular in the West. The USA was distracted by Vietnam and it did not want to damage improving relations between the East and West.

## The Brezhnev Doctrine, 1968

Brezhnev now said communist countries must act together to prevent a communist state from turning capitalist. This was known as the Brezhnev Doctrine. The USSR would continue to control these countries.

## The weakening of the communist bloc

The crushing of the 'Prague Spring' worried Soviet allies. Albania left the Warsaw Pact and the Romanian leader Nicolae Ceauçescu condemned it.

> ### What you need to know
>
> You need to be able to explain why events in Czechoslovakia threatened Soviet rule and how the Soviet Union responded to these events.

> ### Revision tasks
>
> 1 Draw a spider diagram to represent the causes of the 'Prague Spring'.
> 2 Explain the Soviet response to the 'Prague Spring'.
> 3 Why did the 'Prague Spring' not have much effect on Soviet relations with the USA?
>
> TESTED

Exam practice answers at www.hoddereducation.co.uk/myrevisionnotesdownloads

# Exam practice

1 Study Source A below and answer the question which follows:

## Source A

There are many people in the world who really don't understand what is the great issue between the free world and the communist world. Let them come to Berlin! There are some who say in Europe and elsewhere we can work with the communists. Let them come to Berlin!

> US President Kennedy made a speech to a large crowd of people in front of the Berlin Wall, June 1963.

What does Source A tell us about American reactions to Soviet control of Eastern Europe? [4]

2 How did the USSR respond to challenges to its power in Eastern Europe in the 1950s and 1960s?

Use the following guidelines in your answer. You must also use information of your own.
● The Hungarian Uprising, 1956
● Disagreements over Berlin, 1959–61
● Czechoslovakia, 1968 – 'The Prague Spring' [22]

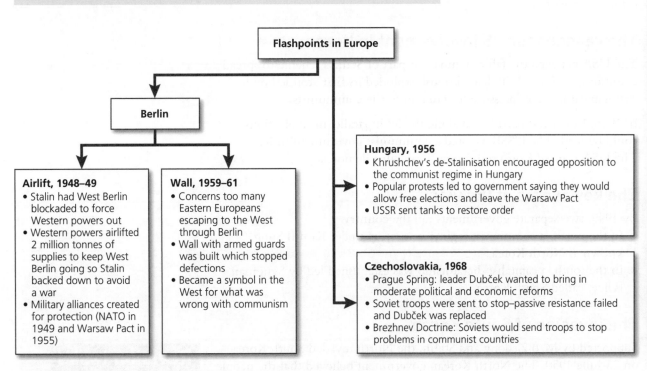

**Summary diagram:** Flashpoints in Europe and the impact on international relations

# 4 Flashpoints outside Europe and the impact on international relations

## Actions of the USA and USSR outside Europe

REVISED

The USA and the USSR both had global influence, so the Cold War spread around the world.

> **What you need to know**
>
> You need to understand how the Cold War spilled out beyond Europe.

## The Korean War, 1950–53

REVISED

### The rule of the USSR

Mao Zedong's Chinese communists had been fighting a civil war with Chiang Kai-Shek's Kuomintang (KMT) since 1927. The USA supported the KMT. In October 1949, Mao's communists won control and established the communist People's Republic of China. In 1950, the USSR committed to supporting China's economic, technological and military development.

> **What you need to know**
>
> You need to be able to explain why the USA became involved in the Korean War and how this affected the Cold War.

### The reasons for US involvement in Korea

The USA believed the fall of China was part of Stalin's scheme to spread communism. The USSR had also just exploded its first atomic bomb. Truman came under pressure to stand up to the communists.

In 1945, Korea was partitioned along the 38th parallel until elections could be held. The USSR wanted a communist government in Korea. The USA wanted Korea to become a capitalist democracy.

### The key events of the war

By 1949, two separate governments ran the country.
- In the north, a communist regime was set up under Kim Il Sung, known as North Korea.
- In the south, a capitalist dictatorship was established led by Syngman Rhee, called South Korea.

### The invasion of South Korea

Supported by Mao Zedong and Stalin, the North invaded South Korea on 25 June 1950. The North Korean government believed that the people of South Korea would welcome them.

### Continuing US involvement

The USA feared a '**domino effect**' would result in the spread of communism. It changed its policy of containment to **rollback** – communism should be attacked and pushed back. The United Nations was asked to stop the attack. The UN condemned the attack and put together a military force to stop the invasion.

> **Revision tasks**
>
> 1 Draw a spider diagram to represent the reasons for American involvement in the Korean War.
> 2 How did the Korean War change the USA's policy of containment?
>
> TESTED

## The UN response

The USSR could not stop any of this as it was boycotting the UN because the USA had refused to allow communist China to sit on the **UN Security Council**. The North Korean Army was about to defeat the South. The UN Army, led by the American General Douglas MacArthur, landed at Inchon in September 1950. It quickly pushed the North Korean Army back to the 38th parallel border between North and South Korea.

## The invasion of North Korea

On 9 October 1950, UN forces crossed into North Korea and went as far as the North Korean border with China, beyond what had been ordered by the UN. MacArthur wanted to reunite the whole country.

## The role of the USSR

The USSR did not enter the conflict because it did not want a world war. It secretly helped the North Koreans and the Chinese with 'advisers', weapons and doctors.

## The role of China

China was afraid the USA wanted to invade them. In November 1950, therefore, 250,000 Chinese troops invaded North Korea and pushed the UN back over the 38th parallel. This was now a war between the USA and China. MacArthur wanted to use the atomic bomb against China. Truman was worried the USSR would get involved, so in April 1951 he sacked MacArthur. The war dragged on and both sides dug in.

## The end of the war

Peace talks began in June 1951 but nothing was achieved. In 1953, Dwight D Eisenhower (1953–61) became US President and Stalin died, to be replaced by Khrushchev. The new leaders sought peace. A ceasefire was agreed at Panmunjom (South Korea) in July 1953. This created a border and a demilitarised zone (DMZ) between the two states.

## The consequences of the Korean War and impact on relations

By the end of the war:
- 2 million people had died
- the border was back where it was before the war
- communism had not spread into South Korea, but rollback had failed
- US–Chinese relations continued to get worse
- the USA signed a peace treaty with, and invested in, Japan
- the USA signed agreements to protect the Philippines, Australia and New Zealand
- NATO was now a full military alliance.

The Korean War indicated that the USA wanted containment anywhere in the world, even if they had to use troops.

### Revision tasks

1 Draw a spider diagram to represent the different reasons for Chinese involvement in the Korean War.
2 Who won the Korean War? Explain your choice.
3 Make a timeline of the causes and main events of the Korean War from 1945 to 1953.

TESTED

# The conflict in Vietnam, 1950–73

Indochina (Vietnam, Cambodia and Laos) had been part of the French empire since 1887, but the French had been beaten by communist **guerrillas** called the Vietminh, who were led by Ho Chi Minh. The 1954 Treaty of Geneva divided Vietnam into the communist North and the non-communist South. The USA worried about the domino effect, that communism could spread through the region.

> **What you need to know**
>
> You need to understand why the USA became involved in the Vietnam War, but also why it failed to achieve its objectives.

## The reasons for US involvement, 1950–64

Eisenhower supported South Vietnam with money, weapons and military advisers to contain the spread of communism. Kennedy (1961–63) increased this support. There were increasing guerrilla attacks against the South by the National Liberation Front (NLF) or Vietcong. They wanted to reunite Vietnam under communist rule.

Ngo Dinh Diem was the unpopular leader of the South. His mostly Catholic government was out of touch with the people, who were mostly Buddhist peasants. The Vietcong gained support. In November 1963, Diem was assassinated.

## The Tonkin Resolution

In August 1964, North Vietnam attacked the *USS Maddox* in the Gulf of Tonkin. Lyndon B Johnson (1963–69) used this attack to increase American involvement in Vietnam. The Tonkin Resolution – passed by Congress – allowed the President to fight the war as he wanted. A large number of American troops landed in Vietnam and the US Air Force bombed the Viet Cong (**Operation Rolling Thunder**). The USA used chemicals like **napalm** which burned civilians and **Agent Orange** which cleared the jungle.

## The actions of the USA, 1965–73

Even though they had more troops, the USA struggled to defeat the Viet Cong because:
- **'Search and Destroy'** tactics focused on the number of the enemy killed, not on beating them
- the USA made mistakes, especially bombing 'friendly' villages
- US soldiers were inexperienced
- Viet Cong guerrilla tactics were effective because they could hide among the peasants
- many Vietnamese people were suspicious of US troops who did not seem bothered about killing them. The most notorious US atrocity was the My Lai Massacre of March 1968.

The morale of the American soldiers fell when they realised the war was unwirrable, while the Viet Cong believed they were fighting a **patriotic** war of liberation.

## The continuing events of the war

In January 1968, the Viet Cong began the Tet Offensive. Their troops got to the South's capital, Saigon, before being driven back. It made Americans feel that they could not win this war.

Television pictures which showed US atrocities and soldiers being brought home in body bags turned the American people against the war. People began to protest against the war. It made President Johnson unpopular but President Nixon (1969–74), his successor, had the same problem, especially after four students were killed at a protest in Ohio in 1969.

## More US actions and the end of the war

Nixon wanted America out of Vietnam, but in a way that did not make them look as if they had lost. He:

- increased the bombing of North Vietnam
- ordered secret bombing raids against Viet Cong supply routes in Cambodia and Laos in 1970
- replaced US troops with South Vietnamese ones from 1969 – this was known as Vietnamisation.

In 1973, the Paris Peace Treaty agreed the withdrawal of US forces. The Viet Cong stayed in the South.

## The role of China and the USSR

China sent soldiers and military equipment to North Vietnam. They built roads, railways and airstrips. Later in the war the USSR trained pilots and gave them modern fighter planes, supplied medicines, food and oil and provided tanks, artillery, anti-aircraft guns and surface-to-air missiles (SAMs).

## The consequences of the war

Many Americans worried about the cost of the war.

- There were heavy military and civilian losses.
- $120 billion had been spent.
- US veterans suffered physical and psychological damage.
- Vietnam was left devastated.

## The impact on relations

- The USA was humiliated and in future was reluctant to send troops into a crisis.
- Containment in Indochina faltered – Vietnam, Cambodia and Laos all became communist.
- Soviet relations with Vietnam were difficult but their military support continued. Vietnam's relations with China worsened because of China's continued aggression in the region.
- The Vietnam War did not destroy the **détente** which was developing between the USSR and the USA in the 1970s.

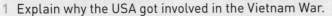

## Revision tasks

TESTED

1 Explain why the USA got involved in the Vietnam War.
2 Make notes on how the USA fought the Vietnam War.
3 Make notes on how the Viet Cong fought the Vietnam War.
4 Make a list of reasons why the USA failed to achieve its objectives in the Vietnam War.

# The Cuban Missile Crisis, 1959–62

The Caribbean island of Cuba is 90 miles off the Florida coast. It nearly became the cause of open war between the USA and USSR in the 1960s.

> **What you need to know**
>
> You need to understand why the Cuban Missile Crisis was one of the most serious events of the Cold War.

## The causes of the crisis

Before 1959, Cuba exported sugar to the USA, while American companies controlled most of the island's industry.

In 1959, Fidel Castro (1926–2016) overthrew the Cuban dictator Fulgencio Batista.

Castro took control of American businesses in Cuba. As the USA stopped trading with Cuba, so Cuba and the USSR agreed to trade oil and sugar for machinery. The USSR became Cuba's main trading partner. In 1961, Castro announced he was a communist.

## The Bay of Pigs

In January 1961, the **Central Intelligence Agency (CIA)** planned to invade Cuba with the help of anti-Castro Cuban exiles. Kennedy approved but it went wrong. Landing at the Bay of Pigs on Cuba, bad intelligence led the invaders to overestimate local support for them. This disaster made Kennedy look inexperienced and turned Castro into a hero.

## Key events: USA and USSR actions

Castro was concerned about the Bay of Pigs invasion and asked the USSR for help. In August 1962, the USSR began to establish nuclear missile bases in Cuba. The missiles would reach most US cities, just like American missiles in NATO member Turkey could reach cities in the USSR.

By 14 October 1962, the USA had photographic proof of these missile bases. They also found Soviet ships were on their way to Cuba with supplies. Kennedy wanted to end this threat.

## The USA's options

ExComm, a committee of the **National Security Council**, advised Kennedy. It considered:
- invading Cuba
- blockading Cuba
- an air attack on the missile bases
- a nuclear attack on Cuba
- allowing the missile bases to be erected.

On 22 October, Kennedy decided on a **naval blockade**. He went on television to explain his decision.

---

## Revision tasks

1 Explain why the Cuban Missile Crisis happened.
2 Draw a timeline of the main events of the Cuban Missile Crisis.
3 Make a list of the consequences of the Cuban Missile Crisis.

**Table 5.3** Timeline of the key events

| Date | Event |
| --- | --- |
| 23 October | The USSR condemned the USA and said it was only helping Cuba defend itself. |
| 24 October | US naval blockade began. |
| | American invasion plan were drawn up. |
| | US Air Force planes flew over Cuba. |
| | Soviet ships were either stopped or turned away at the blockade. |
| 26 October | An America U2 spy plane was shot down over Cuba. |
| | Kennedy received a telegram from Khrushchev – the USSR would remove the missiles if America agreed to end the blockade and not invade Cuba. |
| 27 October | Khrushchev sent a second telegram; it said the USSR would only remove its missiles from Cuba if America removed its missiles from Turkey. |
| | Kennedy decided to ignore Khrushchev's second telegram and agree to the first. |
| 28 October | Khrushchev agreed and began to remove the missiles. |

## Consequences of the crisis and its impact on relations

Nuclear war was avoided. In secret, Kennedy began the dismantling of US missiles in Turkey. Castro remained in power.

Both sides learned to avoid confrontation in the future. A telephone hotline between Washington and Moscow was set up. Talks to reduce the number of nuclear weapons began. The **Partial Test Ban Treaty** was signed in 1963.

## The Soviet War in Afghanistan, 1979–89

REVISED

The early 1970s had seen a softening in relations (*détente*) between the superpowers.

### The reasons for USSR involvement

*Détente* did not last. The USSR was nervous about Afghanistan, a neighbouring country in Asia. It had valuable gas fields, which the Soviets wanted to exploit. It was also a centre of Muslim unrest. Muslim extremists attacked the Afghan government, leading to an uprising in March 1979.

### The actions of the USSR

On 25 December 1979, Soviet forces invaded. By New Year they reached the capital, Kabul, and appointed a '**puppet ruler**'. The invasion was condemned by the United Nations, the USA and China.

Between 1981 and 1987, the American 'Operation Cyclone' supplied guns, missiles and money to the **Mujahideen** – Afghan fighters who waged guerrilla warfare against the Soviet invaders. Many of the *Mujahideen* were Islamic extremists.

The USSR found itself in the same situation as the USA had faced in Vietnam. The *Mujahideen* attacked supply convoys, shot down helicopters and then hid in the mountains. The Soviets could not defeat their enemy. In 1988, the new Soviet leader Mikhail Gorbachev (1985–1991) realised the USSR was not going to win the war. By 1989, he had withdrawn all Soviet troops from Afghanistan.

**What you need to know**

You need to understand why the USSR became involved in Afghanistan, as well as why it eventually left.

**Revision task**

Make a list of the reasons why the USSR did not succeed in controlling Afghanistan.

TESTED

# The short-term consequences of the war and its impact on relations

## The consequences of the war

One million Afghans died and 3 million refugees went to Pakistan. Afghanistan ended up ruled by violent **warlords**.

The USSR went bankrupt and people began to speak out against the Soviet government. **Fundamentalist** Muslim groups like the *Mujahideen* led to international terrorism.

## The impact on relations

The war resulted in:
- a new Soviet communism
- US President Jimmy Carter (1977–81) withdrew from arms reduction talks, stopped trade with the USSR and boycotted the 1980 Moscow Olympics. President Ronald Reagan (1981–89) called the USSR an 'evil empire' in 1983
- more weapons: US nuclear missiles were placed in Europe from 1979 which resulted in protests by peace groups like the **Campaign for Nuclear Disarmament** (CND). Reagan supported the Strategic Defence Initiative (SDI) or 'Star Wars' programme in 1983 to develop lasers to shoot down Soviet missiles. The USSR boycotted the 1984 Los Angeles Olympics.

## Revision tasks

1 How successful was the Soviet invasion of Afghanistan? Explain your answer.
2 What do you think was the most important consequence of the Russian invasion of Afghanistan? Explain your choice.

TESTED

---

**Korean War, 1950–53**
- 1945: Korea divided into North (communist) and South (democratic)
- 1949: Neighbouring China becomes communist
- 1950: The North invades and almost defeats the South
- UN sends US and other troops; North is pushed out of the South all the way to Chinese border
- China attacks UN troops and war becomes a stalemate
- 1953: Ceasefire restores 1945 border

**Conflict in Vietnam, 1950–73**
- 1954: Divided into North (communist) and South (democratic)
- Communist guerrillas in the South, USA sends advisers
- 1964: Gulf of Tonkin attack – large numbers of US forces sent
- USA uses chemical and technological arsenal but fails to defeat communist guerrillas
- 1973: Paris Peace Treaty – USA withdraws from the South
- 1975: Vietnam unified under a communist government

**The actions of the USA and USSR outside Europe**

**Cuban Missile Crisis, 1959–62**
- Castro overthrows Batista dictatorship, begins to nationalise US companies
- USA stops trading with Cuba, Cuba turns to USSR for trade
- Cuba asks USSR for military aid after failed Bay of Pigs attack
- 1962: USSR sends nuclear missiles to Cuba, USA begins naval blockade of the island
- USSR takes missiles from Cuba, USA from Turkey

**Soviet war in Afghanistan, 1979–89**
- 1979: Muslim extremists overthrow pro-Soviet government
- USSR invades and occupies Afghanistan
- USA gives money and weapons to Islamic extremists like the *Mujahideen* to resist Soviet occupation; becomes the USSR's 'Vietnam'
- 1988–9: Soviet forces withdraw from Afghanistan because of lack of success and rising cost

**Summary diagram:** Flashpoints outside Europe and the impact on international relations

# 5 The end of the Cold War, 1985–91

## The actions of the USA and the USSR in Europe and the impact on international relations

REVISED

In the 1980s, the Cold War became more dangerous, but by the end of the decade both sides were co-operating with each other more than they had since 1945.

**What you need to know**

You need to be able to explain why the Cold War got more serious at the beginning of the 1980s, yet came to an end by the close of the decade.

## The role of Reagan

REVISED

Reagan increased military spending, although the cost was so high the American economy began to struggle. When Gorbachev came to power in the USSR in 1985, he withdrew from Afghanistan and ended the Brezhnev Doctrine (see below). Reagan became more diplomatic and negotiated the 1987 Intermediate Nuclear Forces Treaty, but he also made a speech in Berlin calling on Gorbachev to 'tear down this wall!'

## Mikhail Gorbachev: new leader, new policies

REVISED

The Soviet economy was close to total collapse. Gorbachev knew the USSR could not afford to keep up with US spending because:
- living standards were too low
- corruption in the Communist Party meant money was wasted
- millions were starving because of farming failures
- industries needed modernising
- Soviet technology was inferior
- the war in Afghanistan was too expensive.

### Gorbachev's policies: *Glasnost* and *Perestroika*

Gorbachev knew political and economic change was needed if the USSR was to survive. Money was saved by ending the arms race. People had to be free to speak out about what was wrong so things could be improved. His two main policies were:
- *Glasnost* (openness) – freedom to criticise how things were done in the USSR
- *Perestroika* (restructuring) – introducing more capitalist economic reforms.

In 1988, Gorbachev ended the Brezhnev Doctrine. The USSR did not need a buffer zone in Eastern Europe. Gorbachev withdrew Soviet troops from Eastern Europe.

# The collapse of communism in Eastern Europe

In 1989, most Eastern European countries rejected communism. This time there were no Soviet troops to stop them. Even the Berlin Wall fell. The communist government of East Germany tried to stop travel between East and West Germany but the border guards let people through. People climbed onto the Wall and began to demolish it.

**What you need to know**

You need to be able to explain why communist control over the countries of Eastern Europe came to an end in the 1980s.

## The opening of the Iron Curtain

**Table 5.4** The opening of the Iron Curtain

| Country | Key dates | Events |
|---|---|---|
| East Germany | 1989 | November: The Berlin Wall was opened. |
| | 1990 | October: Germany was reunified. |
| Bulgaria | 1989 | November: The Communist leadership resigned. |
| Romania | 1989 | December: Dictator Nicolae Ceausescu fled, but he was executed by the army. |
| Poland | 1989 | June: Anti-communist political party **Solidarity** won elections. |
| | | December: Solidarity's Lech Walesa became President of Poland. |
| Czechoslovakia | 1989 | November: The 'Velvet Revolution' – protesters peacefully ended communist rule. |
| Hungary | 1989 | May: The border with Austria was opened; eastern Europeans could cross into West Germany. |
| | | October: A non-communist government was set up. |
| Baltic States | 1991 | August–September: Estonia, Latvia and Lithuania declared their independence. |
| Yugoslavia | 1990 | Emergence of four different regimes within Yugoslavia. |

## Revision tasks

1 Explain the roles of Reagan and Gorbachev in the end of the Cold War.
2 Construct a timeline showing the main events in the collapse of communism in Eastern Europe.
3 Explain the key events in Eastern Europe that led to the collapse of communism.

# The Cold War ends

Gorbachev knew he needed to cut defence spending. In 1986, he said he wanted to get rid of all nuclear weapons and abandon the Brezhnev Doctrine. Reagan and Gorbachev held **summit meetings**. The 1987 Intermediate Nuclear Forces (INF) Treaty removed 4,000 nuclear warheads and ended the 'Star Wars' programme. Inspectors were to oversee this. In 1988, Gorbachev withdrew Soviet forces from Afghanistan. Troops were also withdrawn from other Iron Curtain countries.

President George H Bush (Senior) (1989–93) met Gorbachev in Malta in 1989. They said the Cold War was over. The Warsaw Pact was disbanded in July 1991.

## Freedom for all?

The USSR was in a state of collapse. Some people wanted more reform, some thought there had been too much already. In August 1991, opponents of change in the Army tried to overthrow Gorbachev. He was soon reinstated by loyalists. He banned the Communist Party and ended the USSR. Fifteen former Soviet countries became independent. Russia, the Ukraine and Belarussia became the Commonwealth of Independent States. Gorbachev resigned on Christmas Day 1991.

> ### What you need to know
> You need to understand how the Cold War came to an end.

> ### Revision task
> Construct a timeline for 1985 to 1991 to represent the events that led to the end of the Cold War.
>
> TESTED

## Exam practice

3  Describe two consequences of the collapse of communism in Eastern Europe. [2+2]

4  How did the Cold War come to an end?

Use the following guidelines in your answer. You must also use information of your own.
- Gorbachev becomes leader of the USSR
- The 1987 INF Treaty
- Soviet withdrawal from Afghanistan [22]

---

**The role of President Reagan**
- Called USSR an 'evil empire' in 1983
- Told Soviet leader Gorbachev to pull down the Berlin Wall in 1987
- Summit meetings with Gorbachev leading to the 1987 INF Treaty

**Policies of Gorbachev**
- *Glasnost*: freedom to criticise
- *Perestroika*: capitalist reforms
- 1988: Ends Brezhnev Doctrine protecting communist regimes
- 1989: Soviet troops leave Afghanistan

**Collapse of communism in Eastern Europe**
- When Gorbachev ended Brezhnev Doctrine protests began against East European governments
- By 1991 all the countries of Eastern Europe had rejected communism

**The Cold War ends**
- 1987 INF Treaty begins to end the arms race
- 1989 Bush and Gorbachev declare Cold War is over
- 1991 Gorbachev ends Warsaw Pact, bans communism, disbands the USSR and resigns

**Summary diagram:** The end of the Cold War, 1985–91

# 6 New tensions emerge, 1991–2003

## The new age of conflict

REVISED

After the Cold War there was a new conflict between Muslim extremists who fought for their religion and Western capitalist democracies. The extremists used terrorism and the West responded with a 'war on terror'.

> **What you need to know**
>
> You need to be able to explain what new challenges to world peace emerged in the 1990s.

## The consequences of the Soviet War in Afghanistan

REVISED

The Soviet withdrawal from Afghanistan left the country in chaos. Brutal warlords took over and fought each other. The *Mujahideen* organised themselves into a powerful international terrorist movement, called the Islamic Unity of Afghanistan *Mujahideen*.

> **What you need to know**
>
> You need to be able to explain how the Soviet War in Afghanistan lead to international terrorism.

### The rise of the Taliban

A *Mujahideen* commander, Mohammed Omar, started to fight the warlords. Because his followers were students in the *madrassas* (Islamic schools) they were called the 'Taliban' (Afghan for 'students'). In 1996, the Taliban took control of Afghanistan and imposed strict **Sharia law** – music, TV, toys and games were forbidden. Women had to wear a **burqa**, could not travel without a man's permission and were not allowed any education. People were punished by execution, stoning, flogging and the cutting off of the hands or feet of thieves.

### The origins of Al-Qaeda

Another extremist group was called the 'Afghan Services Bureau' *Maktab al-Khidamat* (MAK). This group was set up by Osama Bin Laden (see below) and others as a charity to help refugees. The donations actually went towards recruiting, training and arming fighters for the *Mujahideen*.

### Osama bin Laden

Osama bin Laden was the son of a Saudi Arabian billionaire and a devout **Sunni** Muslim. He believed the Muslim world was being attacked by unbelievers. He wanted to destroy all outside influences and follow strict Sharia law. In 1979, he joined the *Mujahideen* in Pakistan and gained a reputation as a hero. He helped remove the Soviets from Afghanistan. After 1989, MAK became the Al-Qaeda organisation – an international network of terrorist groups.

### The Gulf War, 1991

Saddam Hussein, President of Iraq, 1979–2003, used violence to rule his country. The **Kurdish** peoples and others in the north suffered badly. The West saw him as a friend against the fundamentalist Muslim government of Iran. The West supplied Saddam with chemical weapons during the 1980–1988 Iran-Iraq war. In 1990, Saddam invaded Kuwait, a small oil-rich state. US President George Bush Senior organised a coalition which drove the Iraqis out of Kuwait.

 Exam practice answers at www.hoddereducation.co.uk/myrevisionnotesdownloads

## Osama bin Laden's view of the USA

American troops stayed in Saudi Arabia after the Gulf War. By doing so, Osama bin Laden believed the USA was conspiring against Islam – Saudi Arabia was where the Prophet Muhammad had been born in Meccas, Islam's holiest city. In 1998, he issued a **fatwā** (death sentence) against the USA and its allies. Al-Qaeda carried out many terrorist attacks, the largest of which was against the USA in September 2001.

### Revision task

How would you explain the rise of Islamic terrorism in the 1980s and 1990s? Make a list of reasons and then write a sentence for each reason to explain how it led to the rise of Islamic terrorism.

TESTED ☐

REVISED ☐

## Reasons for the September 11 attacks

On 11 September 2001, Al-Qaeda terrorists hijacked passenger planes and flew them into the World Trade Center and the Pentagon. They became known as the '9/11' attacks.

### What you need to know

You need to be able to explain why the September 11 attacks of 2001 happened.

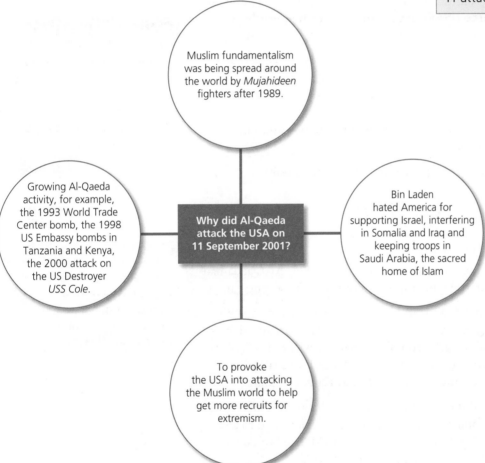

Muslim fundamentalism was being spread around the world by *Mujahideen* fighters after 1989.

Growing Al-Qaeda activity, for example, the 1993 World Trade Center bomb, the 1998 US Embassy bombs in Tanzania and Kenya, the 2000 attack on the US Destroyer *USS Cole*.

**Why did Al-Qaeda attack the USA on 11 September 2001?**

Bin Laden hated America for supporting Israel, interfering in Somalia and Iraq and keeping troops in Saudi Arabia, the sacred home of Islam

To provoke the USA into attacking the Muslim world to help get more recruits for extremism.

## The events of the September 11 attacks

The twin towers of the World Trade Center were a landmark on the New York skyline with 50,000 workers and 200,000 visitors every day. There were four planned attacks:

- two planes flew into the World Trade Center, killing 2,750 people
- a third plane flew into the Pentagon in Washington DC, killing 125 people
- a fourth plane was headed for Washington DC, but the passengers realised this and attacked the terrorists, crashing the plane, killing 40 people.

## The response of the USA and its allies: the 'War on Terror'

The Western world suffered a huge shock. President George Bush Jnr (2001–9) called for a 'War on Terror' to:

- find terrorists like bin Laden and destroy their organisations
- remove governments which supported terrorism
- help countries to resist terrorism by building them into strong democracies
- improve security for US citizens at home and abroad.

The Authorization for Use of Military Force Against Terrorists (AUMF) - passed by congress - gave the President the powers to carry this out, so:

- Afghanistan was attacked and the Taliban regime there was removed by December 2001
- Iraq was invaded in 2003
- 800 terrorist suspects were imprisoned without trial at **Guantanamo Bay**.

The invasion of Afghanistan was undertaken by a NATO **International Security Assistance Force (ISAF)** and the invasion of Iraq was by a coalition from 40 countries. Al-Qaeda leaders began to be found and killed.

In the USA:

- the Department of Homeland Security was created to fight against terrorism
- The Patriot Act (2001) gave the government the right to monitor phone calls and internet messages.

There were more powers for the police to seek and detain suspects.

> ### Revision tasks
>
> 1 Explain the aims of the 'War on Terror', and how they were intended to be carried out.
> 2 List the key events of the 'War on Terror'.
>
> TESTED ☐

## The war in Afghanistan, 2001

REVISED ☐

### Reasons for the invasion

Afghanistan was a centre of Al-Qaeda terrorism. In 1996, Al-Qaeda had moved from the Sudan into Afghanistan, where it set up training camps.

After 9/11, the USA demanded the Taliban government hand over bin Laden and remove Al-Qaeda. On 7 October 2001, America and Britain launched 'Operation Enduring Freedom' – aerial attacks on the Taliban and Al-Qaeda. The International Security Assistance Force (ISAF) removed the Taliban government and put Hamid Karzai in charge.

Mohammed Omar turned the Taliban into a guerrilla army, ambushing ISAF forces with 'attack-and-scatter' raids, suicide missions and roadside bombs. They kidnapped Westerners as well. The ISAF tried to destroy the Taliban but they kept re-grouping and carrying on.

> ### What you need to know
>
> You need to be able to explain why the war in Afghanistan happened and what it meant for international relations.

### The impact on international relations

The war:

- had killed 4,000 ISAF and 15,000 Afghan soldiers and police, as well as 20,000 civilians, by 2016
- had international support from the United Nations
- caused tension in the Middle East – the USA had complaints from Afghanistan about civilian deaths and Pakistan about US military operations inside Pakistan
- caused Muslim anger that increased terrorist recruitment.

> ### Revision task
>
> What do you think the most important reason for the war in Afghanistan was? Explain your choice.
>
> TESTED ☐

# The invasion of Iraq, 2003

REVISED

The West believed Saddam was building up weapons of mass destruction (WMDs) – chemical, biological and nuclear weapons. The United Nations sent inspectors (UNSCOM) to search for them throughout the 1990s. Iraq expelled the UN inspectors in 1997. A few days after 9/11, President Bush tried to prove the connection between Saddam, Al-Qaeda and WMDs. A UN inspection team in Iraq found no evidence of WMDs. Bush told the USA that Saddam could attack them with chemical and biological weapons and his ally British Prime Minister (1997–2007) Tony Blair said the same to UK MPs.

> **What you need to know**
>
> You need to be able to explain why the war in Iraq happened and what this meant for international relations.

## Reasons for the invasion of Iraq

Bush and Blair decided to go to war without getting UN support. They got the support of the US Congress and the British Parliament and attacked Iraq. Bush and Blair said Saddam supported Al-Qaeda and had WMDs, even though there was no evidence of either. It may also be that they wanted Iraq to have a democratic government, that they wanted to control Iraq's oil, or that Bush wanted to finish his father's 1991 war.

## The downfall of Saddam Hussein

The Iraq war began on 20 March 2003 with a '**Shock and Awe**' aerial bombardment. Then American, British and Australian troops invaded, meeting little resistance. The Iraqis were defeated in three weeks. Saddam hid but was captured and eventually hanged. The Coalition tried to build a new democratic Iraq, but faced problems:

- **Shia** Muslims ran the new government which angered the Sunni Muslim majority.
- The US gave rebuilding work to American companies which angered Iraqis.
- Suicide attacks on coalition forces meant westerners had to stay in the fortified 'Green Zone' in Baghdad.
- US troops were accused of abusing Iraqi prisoners.

## The impact of the Iraq War on international relations

Consequences of the war:
- Saddam was overthrown.
- Democratic elections were held in Iraq for the first time.
- There were 50,000 military and over 100,000 civilian deaths.
- There was terrorism in Iraq where there had been none before.

The impact of the war on international relations:
- Several countries, such as Russia, refused to support the invasion.
- There were large protests against the war in many countries, including Britain.
- The **League of Arab States** demanded the immediate withdrawal of US and UK forces.
- Terrorist incidents around the world increased.
- The UN's reputation and authority suffered.

> ## Revision tasks
>
> 1 Explain why the USA and Britain invaded Iraq in 2003.
> 2 How successful was the invasion of Iraq? Explain your choice.
> 3 Make a list of similarities and differences between the wars in Afghanistan and Iraq, including:
>    - reasons for the war
>    - events of the war
>    - consequences of the war for international relations.
>
> TESTED

# Exam practice

**5** Study Sources B and C below and answer the questions which follow:

## Source B

I accept that the Bush Administration made terrible mistakes during the Iraq War, though I still defend the decision to invade Iraq. Many intelligence experts believed that the Iraqis had chemical weapons in their possession and that they would use them against us and their own people.

*The view of an American politician speaking in 2015 about the US invasion of Iraq in 2003.*

## Source C

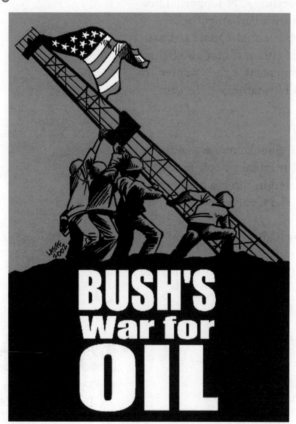

BUSH'S War for OIL

*The view of a cartoonist who was against the US invasion of Iraq in 2003.*

**a** Sources B and C give different views about the reasons for the US invasion of Iraq in 2003. Explain two ways in which these views differ. [2+2]

**b** Explain one reason why the views in Sources B and C are different. [2]

**6** Study Source D below and answer the question which follows:

## Source D

I can say that I apologise for the fact that the intelligence we received about Iraq was wrong. Even though Saddam Hussein had used chemical weapons against his own people and against others, he did not have weapons of mass destruction. Despite this, I find it hard to apologise for removing Saddam Hussein. Even today, in 2015, I think it is better that he is not in power. The invasion of Iraq was part of our war on terror.

> The view of Tony Blair speaking in a television interview in 2015. He was Prime Minister when Britain invaded Iraq in 2003.

How convincing is the view in Source D about the reasons for the British invasion of Iraq in 2003?

Explain your answer using Source D and your contextual knowledge. [8]

**7** Study Sources B, C and D again and answer the question below:

How far do you agree with the view in Source D that the invasion of Iraq in 2003 'was part of our war on terror'?

In your answer, you must use Sources B, C and D and information of your own. [16]

---

**The rise of the Taliban and Al-Qaeda**
- Soviet withdrawal leads to Islamic extremist Taliban taking over
- Former Islamic guerrillas become Al-Quaeda terrorists
- Al-Quaeda leader Osama bin Laden is angered by US troops being stationed in sacred Saudi Arabia in 1991 Gulf War
- Al-Quaeda begin terrorist campaign against the USA and her allies

**11 September attacks, 2001**
- Two planes into World Trade center, New York, one into Pentagon, Washington DC, another plane crashed
- Resulted in USA's 'war on terror' to destroy international terrorism
- New powers for US Government, e.g. Patriot Act

**The 'war on terror'**

**Invasion of Afghanistan, 2001**
- Taliban government supported Al-Qaeda training camps
- Oct 2001: USA and Britain launch Operation Enduring Freedom, an invasion to overthrow the Taliban
- Taliban guerrilla campaign caused a lot of deaths
- Increased international Islamic terrorism

**Invasion of Iraq, 2003**
- USA believed Saddam had chemical and biological WMDs
- USA and Britain invaded Iraq in 2003 after massive aerial 'Shock and Awe' bombardment
- International protests against the invasion
- Saddam overthrown but terrorist campaigns continued

**Summary diagram:** New tensions emerge, 1991–2003

# Notes

Exam practice answers at www.hoddereducation.co.uk/myrevisionnotesdownloads